Grace in Abundance

Grace in Abundance

*Orthodox Reflections
on the Way to Porto Alegre*

World Council of Churches, Geneva

Cover design: Marie Arnaud Snakkers

ISBN 2-8254-1467-0

Printed in France

Table of Contents

Biblical Reflections

Special Commission and Expectations from the Assembly

Foreword

In the years since the eighth assembly of the World Council of Churches in Harare, Zimbabwe (1998), Orthodox participation in the life and work of the Council has constituted a high priority for Orthodox churches themselves, the Council's governing and consultative bodies, and the entire fellowship of member churches.

The Special Commission on Orthodox Participation in the WCC, mandated by the Harare assembly, presented its final report to the central committee in 2002. The almost unanimous adoption of its recommendations as well as the almost immediate implementation of them have created a new spirit within the fellowship, suggested new ways of working together, and opened new avenues for the continuation of the journey on the path of Christian unity.

A tangible sign of these new possibilities, the present volume is a thoughtful Orthodox contribution to the ninth assembly of the WCC, to be held in Porto Alegre, Brazil, in 2006. Representatives of Eastern and Oriental Orthodox churches came together on the apostolic island of Rhodes. Using their rich theological and spiritual resources, they have elaborated an understanding of the assembly theme. Considering the work and recommendations of the Special Commission, they have explored the implications of the forthcoming changes to the life and work of the Council. Attempting a first positive and constructive response to these changes, they have sought ways in which Orthodox churches could strengthen their engagement in the ecumenical movement in general and the WCC in particular.

The present volume could therefore be read as a signpost pointing to the end of a difficult and sometimes painful journey. It confirms that the member churches of the fellowship can resist temptations and overcome difficulties, can transform what looked like an impasse into a new avenue of collaboration. It confirms that, for both Orthodox and other member churches, participation in the Council's life is by no means a matter of "gaining an upper hand", but rather an expression of a serious commitment to the fellowship, a desire to find better ways to witness together and to work together.

There is a powerful description of the ecumenical movement, as a relational reality deeply marked by giving and receiving gifts. In this sense, we receive with joy and gratitude the rich harvest of this inter-Orthodox consultation as a gift of our Orthodox sisters and brothers to the ninth assembly, to the Council and to the ecumenical movement. We particularly value the meditation, a wonderful prayer, concluding the report of the consultation.

Our hope is that our Orthodox sisters and brothers too will receive the many gifts generously offered to them within the fellowship of churches constituting the WCC and discern the many signs confirming how much their participation in the Council's life is cherished and valued.

Samuel Kobia
General Secretary
World Council of Churches

Words of Welcome

Your Eminences, Your Graces,
Beloved Participants,

We welcome you with great joy on behalf of the Ecumenical Patriarchate, the Ecumenical Patriarch Bartholomew and our diocese. We welcome all of you, distinguished hierarchs and eminent theologians, who have come to our island for this important encounter in preparation for the forthcoming ninth assembly for the World Council of Churches which will take place in Porto Alegre, Brazil, in February 2006.

We thank you warmly for having accepted our invitation to come to the island of Rhodes, which – at the crossroads of the Mediterranean and at the crossroads of peoples and civilizations – has always been a venue for ecclesial encounters from ancient times onwards, when ships were carrying bishops from Alexandria, Antioch and Palestine to participate in ecumenical or local councils of major ecumenical interest. The ships came to moor in the harbour of Rhodes and thus afforded the opportunity during the few days of their anchorage (sometimes longer because of bad weather conditions) to discuss various issues on the ecclesial agenda – in other words, pre-conciliar discussions were already taking place at that time on our island.

Since 1960, at the initiative of the Ecumenical Patriarchate, and especially under the particularly fruitful leadership of the late Metropolitan Spyridon, my learned predecessor, pre-conciliar pan-Orthodox meetings were held in this very sacred place, the cathedral of the Annunciation. In these gatherings distinguished representatives of all local Orthodox churches have participated, and these encounters have contributed to strengthen the links between the Orthodox churches after their isolation, which lasted for many centuries because of historical circumstances. When you look around, you will notice distinguished marks and insignia of the Orthodox patriarchates and the autocephalous churches which are still where they were put then as genuine witnesses of those important events that promoted and honoured Rhodes both in the inter-Orthodox and inter-Christian worlds.

Together with the inter-Orthodox encounters this island has also hosted many meetings of the World Council of Churches and other ecumenical encounters, such as the one of Faith and Order in January 1988 where an important document on the apostolic faith was drafted. In November of the same year the significant inter-Orthodox consultation on "The Place of Women in the Orthodox Church and the Question of the Ordination of Women", with the participation of some 100 Orthodox theologians, took place here as well. Many other international fora and encounters have also met here in this historical diocese of the Ecumenical Patriarchate.

The theme of this encounter and of the assembly of the World Council of Churches, "God, in Your Grace, Transform the World", is always actual and very rich from an Orthodox perspective. Our Lord became flesh not simply to offer another teaching, but in order to transfigure humankind and the world. Transfiguration has always been, and still is, the deeper longing of the human being, especially during our era, full of trouble and confusion, a longing which only God's grace, with human cooperation, can fulfil. God's grace, which we implore and for which we pray, is channelled through the Holy Spirit in the life of the church, the sacraments, the creation and each faithful, and is the life-giving force that renews and transforms human beings and the world.

Once again I cordially welcome you and wish that your stay on our island may be a pleasant one and that your encounter and your deliberations will be rich and fruitful by the grace of our great God and our Lord Jesus Christ.

Metropolitan Kyrillos of Rhodes

Preface

Prolegomenon

The ninth assembly of the World Council of Churches is to take as its theme, "God, in Your Grace, Transform the World". At an international pre-assembly meeting of Orthodox member churches in the WCC, convened on the island of Rhodes in Greece in January 2005, participants discussed the spiritual and social dimensions of transformation.

In a comprehensive final report, produced by participants coming from nearly all of the Eastern Orthodox and Oriental Orthodox WCC member churches, the group outlined its theological contribution and hopes for the ninth assembly, which will be held in Brazil in early 2006.[1]

1. Transformation and transfiguration

For the Orthodox, grace is associated with the transforming action of the Holy Spirit in creation. "God's divine unconditional graceful love draws us to him (Rom. 5:15), because humans are not only created by God but they are created *for* God. In God we entirely find the purpose of our lives restored and transformed." The transfiguration of Christ reveals God's ultimate intention for humanity and creation. "Christ gathers all things in him, and the whole of creation is transformed into a new heaven and a new earth."

Spiritual and social transformation are interrelated, the report emphasizes. "The process of the transfiguration of our socio-economic order... involves our

---

[1] The pre-assembly gathering of the Eastern Orthodox and Oriental Orthodox churches is traditionally held prior to WCC assemblies meeting every seven years. There are twenty-two Eastern Orthodox and Oriental Orthodox member churches of the WCC, whose combined membership makes up almost half of the Council's total constituency.

The 2005 Orthodox gathering involving more than fifty hierarchs, clergy and theologians, as well as participants from other WCC member churches, was hosted by Metropolitan Kyrillos of Rhodes on behalf of the Ecumenical Patriarchate from 10-17 January 2005. Metropolitan Gennadios of Sassima (Ecumenical Patriarchate) and Metropolitan Bishoy of Damiette (Coptic Orthodox Church) co-chaired the event. Along with the presentation of a series of theological papers, the programme included prayer, meditations and visits to local communities and monasteries.

personal and communal commitment" and the struggle to forge a "chain of good" affects all aspects of human life.

Recognizing the suffering, violence, injustice and immorality so evident in the world, the participants expressed their conviction that the task of Christians is to call on the action of the Holy Spirit and to act as "fellow-workers" in restoring the "true humanity created in God's image".

2. A renewed council, a renewed commitment

The pre-assembly meeting rearticulated the principles undergirding a continued Orthodox commitment to Christian unity. Referring to ongoing discussions about possible new forms of international ecumenical work, the report affirms that "the world will continue to need a council of churches... an instrument to serve the churches by bringing them into a space for dialogue, shared work, for the mutual exchange of gifts and insights from our traditions, for prayer together".

Participants recognized that "ecclesiology is central to the different understandings of Christian division and Christian unity, and therefore the key to our different approaches to the WCC". The status of other churches in Orthodox self-understanding remains one of the most delicate issues affecting Orthodox participation in the ecumenical movement, and the pre-assembly appealed for further serious study in this area.

3. The Special Commission – a "great promise" for the fellowship

The pre-assembly reviewed the results of the Special Commission on Orthodox Participation in the WCC, established by the eighth assembly at Harare in 1998 to address Orthodox grievances over the direction and priorities of the Council. It underlined the central importance of the Special Commission's findings, which bear "great promise for the whole fellowship", and urged WCC member churches to continue to work on receiving the report, which proposes a series of key reforms to the Council to be presented to the next assembly.

In February 2005, the WCC central committee considered adopting a new method of consensus decision-making as an alternative to the current majority-vote system. "Introduction of consensus... offers the Council a way to reflect the centrality of holy scripture in its life and engage the work of the Council in an atmosphere of openness, trust and humility [and] will enhance the potential for the Council to find its true prophetic voice," the report stated.

But the pre-assembly report acknowledged that the Orthodox churches are faced both with a moment of opportunity and of particular responsibility as a result of the Special Commission, and calls on the Orthodox churches "to continue to make credible expressions of [their] commitment in the character of [their] participation at every level".

4. A prayerful contribution

The report culminates also in the form of a meditation, which is inspired by the theme of the WCC's ninth assembly in Porto Alegre.

The present report, drafted as a contribution to the Porto Alegre assembly, explores the themes of grace and transformation, and concludes on a note of hope in God: "in your grace, you have given us a glorious world – in us it has fallen, in us let it be raised again".

The expression of my respects and gratitude are addressed to His All Holiness the Ecumenical Patriarch Bartholomew, "the great Patriarch of our times", for his hospitality in having hosted this inter-Orthodox meeting in one metropolis of the Ecumenical Patriarchate. His All Holiness is an exceptional church leader and spiritual figure who promotes the dialogue of reconciliation between Christians and churches, inspiring unity, peace and open dialogue with people of other living faiths.

Finally, we also wish to express our thanks and appreciation to all members of the Orthodox task force who had the entire responsibility for organizing this inter-Orthodox pre-assembly meeting, and set the agenda together with recommendations from the Orthodox members of the WCC central committee and others. Our thanks are especially directed to our former colleagues and friends George Lemopoulos, the WCC's deputy general secretary, Teny Pirri-Simonian, moderator of the Orthodox task force, and Renate Sbeghen and Luzia Wehrle, who contributed much to the organization in order to make this meeting possible. A final word of appreciation goes to Metropolitan Kyrillos of Rhodes for his generous hospitality and for his personal efforts in making this meeting a real gathering of Christian fellowship in a spirit of ecclesial love; and particular thanks go to Dr Peter Bouteneff for his kindness in editing the text.

Geneva   *Metropolitan Gennadios of Sassima*
14 September 2005

Report of the Consultation

Preamble

1. By the grace of God, we have gathered here from 10 to 17 January 2005 on the apostolic island of Rhodes to prepare ourselves for the journey to the ninth assembly of the World Council of Churches, meeting under the theme, "God, in Your Grace, Transform the World". We have felt extraordinarily blessed in our encounter with one another.

2. The purpose of this meeting has been to reflect on the assembly theme, to consider the work and recommendations of the Special Commission on Orthodox Participation in the WCC, and to seek ways in which our churches can strengthen their engagement in the movement for the unity of divided Christians.

3. The gathering was graciously hosted by Metropolitan Kyrillos of Rhodes on behalf of the Ecumenical Patriarch, His All Holiness Bartholemew I, to whom we express our profound thanks. During the days of our stay we experienced the true philoxenia (hospitality) of the church and its monasteries, the civil authorities, and the people of Rhodes, who welcomed us into their communities. We witnessed the traces – ancient and modern – of the extraordinary encounter of cultures, faiths and histories in this place.

4. Our meeting brought together more than fifty Eastern Orthodox and Oriental Orthodox participants, theologians, hierarchs, priests, lay persons, young theologians and two representatives from other member churches. Leadership was provided by His Eminence Metropolitan Gennadios of Sassima (Ecumenical Patriarchate) and His Eminence Metropolitan Bishoy of Damiette (Coptic Orthodox Church).

5. We met in the context of daily prayer and fellowship. Our deliberations took the form of meditations on the scriptural passages chosen for the assembly, of papers prepared especially for this meeting, and of plenary and group discussions. During our time together we elaborated our theological and spiritual understanding of the assembly theme, we explored the implications of the forthcoming changes to the life and work of the WCC, and we reviewed the practical preparations for the ninth assembly.

I. Living in a changing world

6. We met at a time when the world was in deep pain about the tsunami disaster that struck down more than 200,000 of our brothers and sisters in Asia and
elsewhere, orphaned tens of thousands of children and rendered millions homeless. Keeping in our hearts and our prayers all those who suffer in this tragedy,
mindful also of the pain of the people in all our contexts, and in particular the
continued conflict in the Middle East, we together pray to the compassionate
Father and Creator of all: God, *in your grace, transform the world*. It was in this
context that we began our reflection on the main theme of the assembly. Our
reflections focused on the transforming grace of God, operating at various levels
of persons, churches, societies, and the creation at large. The spirit of prayer
undergirding the theme prompted us to reflect along liturgical lines, drawing
inspiration from such aspects of the liturgy as offering, invocation of the Holy
Spirit, and commissioning – the sending out into the world.

7. Our intercessory offering of the world in praise and thanksgiving helps us
to present before the Creator God the misery and conflict, injustice and violence
experienced by the vast majority of our brothers and sisters in today's world.
This leads many to pose the perplexing and painful question of human suffering: what does it mean to believe in a loving and compassionate God when millions of people perish or suffer in natural calamities? Although we cannot com-
prehend the inscrutable God, we know that God will ultimately sustain his
creation in his infinite compassion. We also felt that human violence and war and
other man-made disasters of various sorts, were infinitely more brutal and per-
vasive than natural disasters. We are convinced that in offering the world to God
in a liturgical sense involves our deep desire and determination to transform the
world, liberating it from all grief and violence.

8. In the midst of terrible violence imposed on the Latin American people,
on the peoples of the so-called third world in general, strength is given to mobilize, to gather together in solidarity. In the context of tremendous social and economic hardship, they have been strengthened by God in their witness to his transforming power.

9. In calling upon the Holy Spirit of God to indwell and transfigure our lives,
our churches, and our earth, we trust in the Spirit, "who perfects everything that
is and that is to be" (Anaphora, Liturgy of St James). In this work of the Holy
Spirit, in continuing to bring to completion all that is created, we are called to
join synergetically as fellow-workers (1 Cor. 3:9). Thus, our prayer to the Holy
Spirit expresses our commitment to exercise our freedom in cooperating with
the grace of God for the transfiguration of the world.

10. Our service to humanity and the wider creation is a direct expression of
our service to God. Our churches recognize the increasingly multicultural, reli-
giously pluralistic, and secularized contexts in which our faithful live. This
recognition of the new situation requires appropriate pastoral and theological
response. While we know that transformation is a continuous process, our
responsibility to discern the will of God in the ambiguity of history is also an
ongoing task. Our repentance as believers, and as churches, is essentially for this

discernment. Our sense of being sent out to the world to announce the good news of salvation and to heal its wounds provides the motivation and orientation for our gathering, prayers and reflections on the theme "God, in Your Grace, Transform the World".

II. The assembly theme

11. The assembly theme provided the inspiration for reflection on many levels. We took note of the importance of each key word in the theme: God, grace, transformation and world, and sought to give orientation so that these words might be properly understood in the context of the theme.

a. Transformation in scripture

12. Our reflection drew its first inspiration from the Bible. The scriptural account of Christ's transfiguration has a significance which is both existential and eschatological (cf. Rev. 1:14). That which is promised to the righteous in the age to come (1 Cor. 15:5f.) happened to Jesus already in this world. Jesus is the one who brings the new creation. Before the eyes of his most intimate disciples, the human appearance of Jesus was for a moment changed into that of a heavenly being in the transfigured world. This is the anticipation and the hope of the final salvation for all human beings.

13. In this sense the transformation of the world means first of all our own transfiguration. St Paul speaks about Christian people as the "new creation". For his understanding of transformation *(metaschematizo)* or transfiguration *(metamorphosis)* (2 Cor. 3:18; Rom. 12:2) refers to a process, which begins to take place already during the life of this age. Scripture consistently shows how the transformation of the world is a process by which the transcendent eschatological reality of salvation works in the earthly lives of Christians. The signs we are shown of the new creation, which is the grace of Christ's Spirit, leads to the imperative of our response, and points to the world's transfiguration.

b. Grace

14. Grace, like everything referring to God, is trinitarian. The grace of our Lord Jesus Christ, the love of God the Father, and the communion of the Holy Spirit – all is grace. By grace we are justified, by grace we are healed. Yet grace is not only the power of justification. Grace is revealed in all the operations, the energies *(energeia)* of God, his actions, which are of his own free will, i.e. out of love.

15. Grace refers to God's free-will. God creates the world out of nothing, as an act of grace rather than necessity, and he also recreates it – he transforms it through his Son Jesus Christ – by his grace, rather than out of necessity. We do not exist without God's grace, his love, and his constant sustaining of the world by his Holy Spirit "by which we live and move and have our being" (cf. Acts 17:28).

16. Furthermore, it is by grace that God gives us the church, in which we are called to live in unity in Christ. Unity in the church is unity-in-plurality, as mod-

elled by the Holy Trinity. Our partaking of that unity here and now is a foretaste of our partaking of the divine nature – our calling to holiness, and deification *(theosis)*.

c. The transformation of our lives

17. We believe in God who sent his Only-Begotten Son, Jesus Christ, and through him reconciled the world to himself, and by the Holy Spirit offers new and eternal life to all. Our Christian life is sustained by the power of the Holy Spirit in the vivifying and sanctifying fountain of grace. The ultimate vocation and supreme goal of all human persons is theosis (2 Pet. 1:4). As St Athanasius the Great has said, "God became human in order that we may become divine."

18. God's divine unconditional graceful love draws us to him (Rom. 5:15), because humans are not only created by God but they are created for God. In God we entirely find the purpose of our lives restored and transformed by his gracious presence (2 Pet. 1:3). In this respect it is our universal priestly vocation to bring the whole world to God – through ethical choices in a community bound together in faith and worship (John 4:23). We act in a fellowship of sharing and service as our response to the emerging political and social challenges. The genuine Christian faith is a practised faith in words and deeds as witness and mission.

d. Transformation in the churches

19. Jesus Christ, who is "the same, yesterday, today, and forever" (Heb. 13:8), is the head of the church, which is his body, sustained by the Holy Spirit, and in this sense the church cannot sin. Therefore we do not ask for the "transformation of the church". However, if we are referring to "the churches" specifically in the sense of communities of believers in history, we know full well that believers sometimes fail to actualize the true being of the church. It is we sinners, personally and in community, who require transformation. The transformation in the churches is a transformation, which we must live out in our lives personally and as communities.

20. The word *koinonia*, which has seen ever-increasing use in ecumenical circles, is another concept which admits several meanings. In its fullest sense it describes a communion which has its centre in the Holy Trinity, and sacramentally in the holy eucharist. In this case one cannot describe the fellowship of the churches within the WCC as koinonia. On the other hand the fellowship of the churches in the WCC confessing together Jesus Christ as Lord and Saviour in the love of the Father and the fellowship of the Holy Spirit, does have a spiritual quality, a deep Christian content, in ways which still need to be explored and spelled out.

e. The transformation of our societies

21. Again and again in our reflections on transformation we returned to the transfiguration of Christ, which has clear implications for the transfiguration of humanity and of the whole creation. The transfiguration of Christ, which shows God's ultimate intention for the world, has been used as a paradigm for a call to

a renewed and transforming missionary ethos and commitment in the Orthodox churches. As members of Christ's body, the church, filled with the grace of the Holy Spirit, who is a witnessing Spirit (Mark 13:11; John 16:13), we are called by an inner compulsion (Acts 4:20) to be his witnesses to the end of the world, to be the "little leaven which leavens the whole loaf" (Gal. 5:9), and his co-workers (1 Cor. 3:9) until Christ gathers all things in him, and the whole of creation is being transformed into a new heaven and a new earth.

22. Transfiguration has also become a key reference point in the Orthodox tradition for theological-ethical reflection: ours is a transfigurative ethic. Our ethics entail rediscovering our true humanity created in God's image, particularly in the face of contemporary attempts to manipulate and cheapen human nature. The injustice, violence and immorality which reign in our world, disfigure the true form of God's world. The process of the transfiguration of our socio-economic order and human relations involves our personal and communal repentance, and our commitment to struggle against the global vicious circle of evil in our world and replace it by the chain of good. Healing, hospitality, "holistic localness" and communion are some of the key elements in transfigurative ethics. This requires a renewed attention and practical follow-up on the part of Orthodox churches.

f. The transformation of the whole creation

23. Orthodox theology of creation is clear about the responsibility of humankind towards the creation of God, where human persons are called to become its guardians, as sons and daughters of God. In the Orthodox church we constantly pray for God's creation – for seasonable weather, for the abundance of the fruits of the earth. Furthermore, we experience the sanctifying character of our sacramental acts, such as the blessing of the waters, and the blessing of bread, of oil, of the physical elements of creation. This is because we recognize that with us and through us, creation has fallen away from its glory, and "groans in travail" awaiting transformation. In one of our vesperal hymns (Tone 7, Monday) we sing:

> I have become an object polluting the earth, air and water,
> for I have stained my body, soul and mind with deceptions...

Since we human beings are created as a "microcosm", encompassing both the physical and the spiritual, what we do and how we act has a profound bearing on the whole of creation. Both the fall and the transformation of creation take place in us and through us.

24. We are therefore all the more challenged to respond to the ecological and environmental problems of our world today, in the light of our theology and liturgical life, with concrete and practical actions. It is in this spirit, and with this sense of our own personal and communal responsibility, that we ask God, in his grace, to transform the whole creation.

25. Our reflection on the theme consistently relies on our understanding of our own personal and communal responsibility for the fall of creation, and expresses the personal and ethical dimension of the transformation, which we

beg of God. Our prayer to God that He transform the world is not a plea that He would change things to be better, that we might wake up one day to find ourselves in a renewed world. It is a plea that He would work in us and through us, call us to receive, realize and enact that transformation which He has already wrought in his Son, Our Lord, God, and Saviour Jesus Christ.

III. The Special Commission

a. *Looking towards the future*

26. We reflected on the work, the ethos and the report of the Special Commission on Orthodox Participation in the WCC. We wish to begin here by expressing our profound gratitude to all the churches in the WCC, and most especially to those who participated in the Commission, to those who have engaged with it. The creation and work of the Commission was justified – indeed, it was long overdue. Yet we deeply appreciate the patience and care with which our partners listened to us.

27. The Special Commission was created by the eighth assembly at Harare in December 1998. This was a response to the crisis in Orthodox relations with the WCC in the 1990s. Regrettably, two Orthodox churches had left the Council, and in other Orthodox churches there was a growing sense of alienation. Although the crisis in Orthodox participation had become acute and inescapable during the last decade of the 20th century, there had been difficulties and tensions from the beginning of the WCC's journey.

28. The theological presuppositions, organizational structure and ethos of the WCC issued largely from the experience of Western Christianity. It was this Western perspective which became the "ecumenical norm". The Orthodox convictions and perspectives were inevitably heard as critiques coming from a minority, usually respected or at least tolerated, but not affecting or changing the normative approach of the majority.

29. The response of the WCC came at the Harare assembly in the form of the creation of the Special Commission, whose mandate was to assess and discuss the WCC's "structure, style and ethos", with a view towards making proposals for overcoming the crisis.

30. The Special Commission was begun with great enthusiasm and expectations. One might say that the outcome of the Commission was more "ecumenical" than "Orthodox", and this has required the adjustment of our expectations. But we realize that this will mean a more lasting and a more genuine solution for the Council as a whole. Indeed, we affirm without reservation the work and recommendations of the Special Commission, its report in all its aspects.

31. At our meeting we gave particular space to two aspects of the report: matters of ecclesiology and the change in process of the conduct of meetings to consensus. However, we also took careful note of the report's other major sections. Regarding social and ethical issues as addressed by the Commission, we are hopeful that a shift to consensus discernment will offer to the Council a highly promising way to grapple with such issues. Regarding common prayer,

we are pleased that the Council has already been implementing the proposed framework, and commit to continue to work together towards a common prayer life that is reflective of ecumenical realities. Recommendations for adjustments to the current policies for membership were heard with appreciation, particularly the introduction of theological criteria for new applicants for membership and the addition of a new mode of relating to the Council.

32. Although the Special Commission no longer meets, its recommendations, adopted by the central committee (August 2002), have only just begun to be put into practice, and will truly begin at the ninth assembly. We have every confidence that these recommendations bear great promise for the whole fellowship, as long as they are given a real chance to work. We appreciate that attention to these issues will continue in the life of the WCC through the Permanent Committee on Consensus and Collaboration, so that the Orthodox churches will no longer experience the kinds of frustrations that led to the formation of the Special Commission.

33. Naturally, we have a lot at stake in the results of the Special Commission. We hope that our insistence on its recommendations is understood properly: it reflects a concern for the ecumenical movement and for the WCC that is its privileged instrument. As former WCC general secretary Konrad Raiser has put it, "The action adopted by the central committee is by no means a matter of either Orthodox or Protestant churches gaining an upper hand." It reflects serious frustrations and dissatisfactions, yes, but it also arises from a commitment to the fellowship, and therefore the desire to find better ways to work together. We hope to continue to make credible expressions of that commitment in the character of our participation at every level, including, where possible, our increased financial contribution.

b. Ecclesiology

34. We were pleased by the Special Commission's attention to matters of ecclesiology. The report is justified in seeing ecclesiology as central to the different understandings of Christian division and Christian unity, and therefore the key to our different approaches to the WCC.

35. We took notice of the particular question posed to the Orthodox in the Special Commission report: "Is there space for other churches in Orthodox ecclesiology? How would that space and its limits be described?" This question follows naturally from our self-understanding – specifically in our self-identification with the one, holy, catholic and apostolic church.

36. Orthodox theologians began to confront this question systematically mainly since the beginning of the 20th century, influenced by the ecumenical movement – the new forms of bilateral dialogues, as well as the unprecedented multilateral encounter with other churches. Since then, many have reflected and written on the subject, but have yet to find coherence in their conclusions. Here in Rhodes we began a fruitful discussion on the question, and expressed the clear desire to pursue it carefully and systematically together. The means of this study process is not yet clear. While it could find a home in the ecclesiology work of the Faith and Order Commission, as the Special Commission report suggests,

we believe the process would best begin among ourselves. We are convinced that such a study is necessary and timely, both in response to the respectful challenge posed us by the Special Commission, and also in order to achieve a greater clarity and consistency regarding this question among our own churches. This is all the more vital, given the increasingly pluralistic context in which our churches live today.

c. Consensus

37. We recognize that the shift in the process of making decisions from a parliamentary voting system based on "majority rule" to a system designed to discern consensus will be among the most visible results of the Special Commission. This shift is designed to remedy the perennial problem of the Orthodox churches as a minority in the World Council of Churches, which is not reflective of church realities. However, the implications of the shift are far greater than redressing this historical imbalance. Scripture itself illumines the way towards this model. St Paul encouraged the Corinthians, "Now, I appeal to you, brothers and sisters, by the name of our Lord Jesus Christ, that all of you be in agreement, and that there be no divisions among you, that you be united in the same mind and the same purpose" (1 Cor. 1:10).

38. The premise of the composition of the Special Commission was that of parity or equal footing (50 percent Orthodox and 50 percent from the other churches of the fellowship) and some anticipated that this model would be recommended for all meetings and governing bodies. In fact, the parity model has proven extremely helpful for the Special Commission itself, as well as for other committees and meetings, such as the meeting on social and ethical issues (Morges, October 2003), and has been affirmed in the composition of the Permanent Committee on Consensus and Collaboration.

39. Introduction of consensus as the primary method within the life and work of the WCC offers the Council a way to reflect the centrality of holy scripture in its life, and engage the work of the Council in an atmosphere of openness, trust and humility, where the views of all churches will be encouraged and listened to with respect. We trust that the change to consensus will enhance the potential for the Council to find its true prophetic voice, and may offer a model that invites to the Council churches of that vast Christian constituency not yet members of the Council (including the Roman Catholic Church).

40. We emphasize our realization that undertaking the work of the Council through consensus discernment and decision-making will challenge all of us; it will require our learning new ways of being together. It will entail a deep spiritual commitment that will challenge all member churches of the Council. All participants will have to commit to being attentive and respectful listeners to the voices and positions of all churches, as this method privileges no one. The consensus method is not an end in itself, but has emerged as the best way forward for discerning the direction of the Council and deepening the fellowship of the churches. Understanding that return to the status quo is no longer tolerable, we welcome this new method of conducting the life of the Council with hope.

*d. The fellowship of churches and the ecumenical movement
   in the 21st century*

41. We were informed about new efforts to look at the ecumenical movement in the 21st century. We are aware both of the structural and financial challenges the ecumenical movement is facing today. However the ecumenical movement is reconfigured, the world will continue to need a council of churches, i.e. a council which brings together Christian bodies who understand themselves as churches. The world needs an instrument to serve the churches by bringing them into a space for dialogue, for shared work, for the mutual exchange of gifts and insights from our traditions, for prayer together, and to express our commitment to unity.

42. We believe further that such a council, precisely as a fellowship of churches, will properly operate along precisely the kinds of recommendations made by the Special Commission report: it will account for the ecclesiological issue and respect ecclesiological neutrality; it will foster prayer that reflects the real situations and convictions of the churches; it will be theologically serious in every way, including the way in which it considers churches applying for membership; it will operate on consensus at every level.

IV. A meditation

O merciful God,
by your eternal Son and by your Holy Spirit,
You have created the world out of nothing.
You have brought all things from non-existence into being,
not out of necessity, but in your free will,
out of your own loving-kindness, in your grace.
You have created the world in which You were well pleased.
As the crown and fulfilment of creation, You made us, human beings,
whom You endowed with your own image, after your own likeness,
to delight in the world and in your glory.
But we abused our freedom,
we have distorted your image, and became alienated from your living
      presence.
Through us and with us, the whole of creation is also fallen.
Yet You have not turned away from the world which You love.
In your own free will, in your mercy and loving kindness,
You have sent your Son to redeem the world,
to transform the world,
to recreate the world.

In your Son, our Lord and God and Saviour Jesus Christ, You have renewed us.
Yet we continue to deny this gift.
We fall away, and need to be called back in repentance.
We have distanced ourselves from You:
do not remember our sinfulness!

Call us again, so that we might be returned to You,
until You have brought us into your kingdom which is to come,
until You have made us to be partakers of your nature.
In your grace, You have redeemed us by your Son in the Holy Spirit:
O God, in your grace, transform our lives!

In your Son and by your Holy Spirit,
You have granted us the church – the body of Christ,
which You have made to be one, holy, catholic and apostolic.
In your church we experience your kingdom which is to come.
In your church we experience the redemption, transformation, recreation of the
    world.
In your church we are healed and reconciled.
By your Holy Spirit, keep us faithful to the unity, holiness, catholicity and
    apostolicity of your church.
Call us to repentance, to transformation, that we may truly be your church.
In your grace, You have given us the holy church:
O God, in your grace, transform us for the sake of your church!
In your Son, who was transfigured in front of his disciples,
You showed us the divine brightness of the uncreated grace,
You showed us that the one who would be crucified is life and light.
In your Son, who emptied himself, taking the form of a servant,
and went to his voluntary life-giving death,
You have taught us that the way to transfiguration is to love one another – even
    our enemies – as ourselves,
to take up our cross daily,
to be servants of one another.
In our pettiness, our pride, and our lust for power,
we demean each other's dignity,
we lose sight of your image in each other,
we wound and break each other with violence.
Call us to repentance, to witness to the world, to transformation.
**In your grace, You have given us all that we require to live together in
    harmony and justice,**
O God, in your grace, transform us for the sake of the world!

You have given us a world to delight in,
the manifestation of your own uncreated glory,
and gave us the charge to till it and keep it,
to exercise a responsible stewardship over all living things and the whole
    creation.
You have given us the examples of your saints,
whose relationship to the animals and to nature prefigures the new life, when
    the lion shall lie down with the lamb.
But in our callousness, we have mistreated animals, and brought many to
    extinction.

In our greed and our short-sightedness,
we have squandered the resources of the world,
we have razed forests,
we have poisoned the air and the waters.
We threaten ourselves, each other, and future generations,
and we offend your glory.
Because of our sin, the whole of creation groans in travail, awaiting
　　transformation.
**In your grace, You have given us a glorious world – in us it has fallen,
in us let it be raised again:**
O God, in your grace, transform the whole creation!

"God, in Your Grace, Transform the World"

An Orthodox Approach*

METROPOLITAN PROF. DR GENNADIOS OF SASSIMA

The end of the 20th century was marked by an obsessive compilation of retrospective listings, assessing the most significant events and moments as well as the most important personalities of the previous century. Some observers – among them Philip Jenkins, the famous American contemporary historian of religions, still more ambitious – tried to identify the high and low points of the whole millennium. Yet in almost all of these efforts, religious matters as well as ecumenical trends received remarkably short shrift. [1] When religious personalities were highlighted, they were usually those who can be most closely identified with secular political trends. Martin Luther King Jr is an obvious example, but there are also others. But why are we referring to the religions? After all, the attitude seemed to be in recent years that religious change could not possibly compete in importance with the major secular trends, movements like fascism or communism, feminism or environmentalism, etc. On the contrary, it is precisely the religious changes that are the most significant, even the most revolutionary, in the contemporary world that influenced and also considerably affected the worldwide ecumenical family and ecumenism in particular.

Christianity also today is living in a rapidly changing world. We are facing all kinds of changes – there are still wars, there are acts of terrorism everywhere, poverty and famine still reign, infractions of human rights and injustice still exist, and all the ills that human beings have known in every age and time. But we also face changes that are more far-reaching and at times portentous. The future may well be very different from what we can imagine in our churches, and it certainly will be very different from what past generations have imagined. However, we already have some experience of such changes in our everyday life as a host of new words and expressions have entered our daily life in the past few years: internet, cyberspace, "virtual community", genetic engineering, globalization, New Age and many more. Meanwhile, ten new countries have enlarged the European Union, and other candidates are thinking of joining. Discussions are taking place at the constitutional level in Europe on Christian roots and

---

* Parts of this paper were published in *The Ecumenical Review*, vol. 56, no. 2, July 2004, pp.285-93.

values. These changes affect our ecumenical life and challenge the ecumenical movement in particular.

Since the Harare assembly in 1998, the World Council of Churches has faced numerous changes, and the report of the Special Commission on Orthodox Participation in the WCC has led to proposals for further constitutional changes, but not only that. The churches – and the Orthodox in particular – are expecting and hoping that something "spectacular" may happen at the next WCC assembly. However, we are living with the hope which is "dying at last". How are we envisioning the future? What are we looking for? For a new and transformed world? Or a transfigured world based upon Christian and human values? Is this the reality or merely a human utopia? As we approach the next WCC assembly in Porto Alegre, Brazil, under the theme "God, in Your Grace, Transform the World", the Christian churches once again are invited to reflect, react and respond to the theme. The following reflections are a contribution from a theological point of view and from an Orthodox perspective. It is obvious that in this short paper these reflections cannot cover all the aspects, perspectives and expectations of the proposed theme.

An Orthodox voice and witness to the world...

How is Orthodoxy to respond to this changing world and to the challenges facing the ecumenical movement in general and the World Council of Churches in particular? A first and most obvious answer is how God's grace is acting and might transform the existing world through our faith and belief, and how our churches might respond to the need for the world to be transformed as the ultimate goal of the fulfilment of God's plan for our salvation. How is it possible to reconfirm once more that "the faith once delivered to us", expressed by Jesus Christ, remains "the same yesterday, today and forever" (Heb. 13:8), that we remain steadfast in the Tradition which has sustained us and our Christian churches through the ages? But we should not let our love of the past and our nostalgia for the past cause us to forget another obvious and important truth: that Christ sent his followers into the world to "make disciples of all nations" (Matt. 28:19) and to proclaim the Word in each new cultural context. Orthodox teaching addresses a host of questions that would have been unimaginable generations ago. It must faithfully proclaim the word of God, but in ways that will embrace all the new words – and the realities behind them – that we encounter and use in our life today, our sense of values, our attitude towards our fellow human beings and our relationship with God. How is Orthodoxy to respond to this new historical, social and cultural situation? Do we have a timely theological word to offer?

The world needs the full richness of Orthodox theology in all its aspects and manifestations, not simply routine repetition of verbal formulas, however laudable these may be. Our various theologies often speak about the dignity of the human person, made in the image and likeness of God. But how often do we forget about this when we are debating theological issues! We must be courageous enough to speak the truth, but we must do so in love.

Let us follow the example of the apostle Paul, who in dealing with the Corinthians was determined "to know nothing... except Jesus Christ, and him crucified" (1 Cor. 2:2). The message of "Jesus Christ, and him crucified" is scandal enough, foolishness enough, without our own contribution. But we also are reminded that in the cross lies victory – the victory not of passing empires but of God's kingdom, whose power is meant to extend to every corner of the world. Today our churches have to witness "Jesus Christ, and him crucified" and to share in the hidden power of God's grace, which is expressed in the energy of the Holy Spirit in all ecclesial life.

"Holy Spirit" and "grace"

The Orthodox Church, in its broad teaching about "grace" [2] (χάρις) or about "divine grace" (θεία χάρις), as it is expressed literally in its confessional statements of faith and in its dogmatic texts, places "grace" in the context of its teaching about the Holy Trinity. Thus, in its teaching about God the Father, all that God provided man, *anthropos*, from the creation of the first Adam until the coming of his incarnate Son and Word in the world is placed within the broad *grace* of God the Father.

Later, all that Jesus Christ the incarnate Word of God did for the salvation of the human race, from his incarnation to his sacrifice on the cross, his resurrection, his ascension, and until the day of Pentecost – all this is placed in the salvific grace of Christ.

Consequently, all the energies ἐνέργεια of the Paraclete, the Holy Spirit, from the day of Pentecost until the end of times ἔσχατα, the Orthodox church places in the sanctifying and perfect grace of the Holy Spirit. Through these energies, humanity realizes human perfection in holiness and growth into a life with Christ in the church and its sacraments, and is guided to full communion and union with God. [3]

As such, grace is manifested by God, but not transmitted to humankind, as if it were an actually existing entity. When St Paul says, "by grace you have been saved" (Eph. 2:5), he is declaring the forgiving love of God by virtue of which the repenting sinner has access to the Holy Spirit. [4]

"Grace" does not refer to itself, but to the Spirit which is given to humankind of divine favour. It speaks of the pardon that God pronounces upon sinful man when he repents in faith. When it is stated in scripture that grace is given or received, this means that the human being becomes the recipient of divine pardon and absolving goodness, not as a super entity added to our basic human nature, but as expressed in the growth of humankind's communion with the Spirit.

"Grace" is also not a new concept in the New Testament, associated only with the atoning death of Jesus Christ. [5] Creation itself is an expression of divine favour and love. "What belongs to the law was itself the work of grace," St John Chrysostom teaches, "as well as our very creation out of non-existent things, since not for our preceding good deeds did we receive such a recompense." [6] Humankind exists *"by grace"* and not *"by nature"*. As St Macarius the Egyptian states, "the very fact that he is man he enjoys by grace *(kata charin)*". St

Paul's doctrine of grace begins from the position that the whole life of salvation rests upon God's mercy or free gift. Power, happiness, peace, achievement and bliss are conditional upon open-hearted receptivity towards God through the self-surrender of faith. Through the generous love or gift of God in grace, salvation is bestowed and a new world of blessings is opening. A world transformed to a new reality. Man is saved, not by anything proceeding from himself or from his own nature. Salvation proceeds from God and is exhibited in the cross of Christ.

"Grace", consequently, is not the power itself, as such, which effects justification in the sinner, but the Holy Spirit that indwells in the sinner's heart in greater abundance by virtue of God's grace. According to St Diodorus of Tarsus, "the operation of the Spirit can be called 'Spirit'. We can also call the Spirit 'operation' *(energeia)*." St John of Damascus likewise holds that "the Spirit is understood in many ways. The Holy Spirit and the powers of the Holy Spirit are known as 'spirit'."

In certain instances in the scriptures, the redeeming power which humankind receives from God is called "grace" and sometimes simply "the Holy Spirit". It is the Spirit, as God, that is operating for human redemption, and not some impersonal power originating from God. Whether we call it "grace" or "energy", the fact remains that we are referring to the living, personal presence and indwelling reality of God's Holy Spirit in humankind.

When we say that humanity exists by "grace" and not by nature, we mean that we exist by virtue of the Spirit in which we live, move and have our being, be we godly or ungodly. The Spirit is like the "oxygen", so to speak, in which the soul subsists and breathes. Likewise, when we say we are saved by grace, we mean we are redeemed by Christ who releases his Holy Spirit in super abundance into humankind's soul.

The exact and discriminate meaning of the word grace should be crystal clear to every man, *anthropos*, of God. With such insight only can he feed his own soul on the inexhaustible riches which it unfolds, and with such understanding only can he be enabled clearly to pass on to others its marvellous, transforming theme. Here is a striking illustration of the fact that a great deal may be represented by one word. When used in the scriptures to set forth the grace of God in the salvation of sinners, the word *grace* discloses not only the boundless goodness and kindness of God towards humankind, but reaches far beyond and indicates the supreme motive which actuated God in the creation, preservation and consummation of the universe in the fulfilment of the worship. What greater fact could be expressed by one word?

Spirit and grace in the liturgy

Orthodox worship, or "liturgy", is always identified to be a worship in gathering, that is, a worship within the synaxis of the community. The individual joining the community for worship and prayer is a personal act. It is a human response to the divine call.

For Orthodoxy, theology, and especially trinitarian theology, is wholly confessional, that is, doxological in character and soteriological in its importance.

The worship of God as Trinity is a dynamic and soteriological experience of the grace of God, the beauty of God experienced in the liturgy of prayer, and is expressed in the church's confession of praise. The worship of the church reflects the mystery of the Christian existence. Worship is, and is to be, determined by the doctrinal faith, that is, by the believing insight into the object of worship, God. As Georges Florovsky states, "Christians worship on the basis of their creed, and it is in the light of devotional experience and evidence that the creed itself assumes its full existential validity and significance, as a committed witness of faith in God's grace."

Worship primarily and essentially is an act of praise and adoration. This implies a thankful acknowledgement of God's embracing love and redemptive loving kindness.

The church, on the other hand, in worship, especially in the *epiclesis* offered in the Divine Liturgy of St John Chrysostom, clearly reveals to us the doctrine of the Holy Trinity. We read:

> Once again we offer to Thee this spiritual worship without the shedding of blood, and we ask, pray and entreat thee (Father): send down thy Holy Spirit upon us and upon these gifts here presented.
>
> And make this bread the precious Body of thy Christ and that which is in this cup thy precious blood of thy Christ. Amen.

The glorification of God is trinitarian in essence and the community offers spiritual worship to the Father, the Son and the Holy Spirit. St Gregory the Theologian demonstrates the doxological expression of the Trinity in the following words: "Adorable unity in trinity, and trinity recapitulated in unity; entirely venerable, entirely regal, of the same throne and glory, transcendent and timeless, uncreated, indivisible, untouchable, uncircumscribable". [7]

St Paul, in Romans 8:26-27, teaches that the Spirit's inspiration of prayer transcends words, since the realities encountered in worship are beyond the limited scope of reason, the longing for the divine communion which is inexhaustible for the rational mind. The very purpose of life is to worship the transcendent mystery as revealed by the incarnate Christ.

The starting point of patristic and Orthodox epistemology is clearly stated by Fr John Romanides, one of the outstanding contemporary theologians, in the following statement: "is the partial knowability of the divine actions or energies and the absolute and radical unknowability and incommunicability of the divine essence. This is not as a result of speculative meditation but of the personal experience or participation in the uncreated glory of God." [8]

The church as the community of God has the mission to be in the world and by its presence and the manner of its existence to confess, praise and glorify the Holy Trinity. The unity of the church as a worshipping community as in the manner of the Trinity enables it to partake organically in the divine and blessed life, that is, receiving the "grace" of the Comforter and becoming witness to God the Holy Trinity who loves the world. Fr Florovsky used to say in class that he or she who has really seen the church has seen the Holy Trinity. It is a vision revealed to those who are baptized in the name of the Holy Trinity. St Maximos the Confessor emphasized those "who have attained not only union with the Holy Trinity, but also the unity which can be perceived within the Holy Trinity".[9] Theology is a real mystery delivered to the church. It is not an intellectual or speculative concern of the individual philosopher or theologian. Dogma serves as a guide for each life of the Christian, it is the truth that sets us free. It is the mysterious presence of God that surpasses all understanding.[10]

The Orthodox ontology of the person is rooted in the holy scriptures, and the ontological dimension of the person is the expression of the church's faith in the triune God. The debate of the three hypostases of God gave rise to the question: What is the meaning of the statement, "God is Father, Son and Holy Spirit" and at the same time, "God is one"? This led to the identification of the hypostasis with the person. That is, the being of God has three modes of existence and the cause and principle of the divine hypostases is the Father. Metropolitan John of Pergamon strongly affirms that "outside the Trinity there is no God, no divine substance, because the ontological 'principle' of God is the Father. The personal existence of God (Father) constitutes his substance – makes it hypostasis. The being of God is identified with the person."[11]

This is not the Heideggerian understanding of ontology but rather the patristic view of the ontology of the person as hypostasis. The Orthodox understanding of the ontology of the person is expressed in love.[12] The human person in relation to God is personal and this relation is manifested in love as God's energy and "grace". God's love is expressed in his "image" that is, the close relation of God as lover and the human person as the "beloved". So the ontology of persons is grounded in relations fulfilled by God's grace and accomplished in the church.

The church as new creation: the cosmic and the eschatological

Such an attempt must probably begin with the church as new creation. Orthodox ecclesiology traditionally sees the beginning of the church in paradise and its life as the manifestation of the kingdom of God. Metropolitan Philaret of Moscow wrote, "The history of the church begins with the history of the world. The very creation of the world can be seen as preparation for the creation of the church because the end for which the kingdom of nature was established is in the kingdom of grace." Thus, the basic dimensions of Orthodox ecclesiology where God's grace is revealed are *cosmic* and *eschatological,*[13] according to Fr Alexander Schmemann.

On the one hand, in Christ, the incarnate Son of God, the new Adam, creation not only finds redemption and reconciliation with God, but also its fulfilment. Christ is the Word, the Logos, the Life of all life, and this life, which was lost because of sin, is restored and communicated in Christ, in his incarnation, death, resurrection and glorification, to humanity and through us to the whole creation. The event of Pentecost, the descent of the Holy Spirit, the giver of life, is not a mere establishment of an institution endowed with specific powers and authority. It is the inauguration of the new age, the beginning of life eternal, the revelation of the kingdom, which is "grace, joy and peace in the Holy Spirit". The church is the continuing presence of Pentecost as power of sanctification and transfiguration of all life, as *grace, which* is knowledge of God, communion with him and, in him, with all that exists. The church is the creation as renewed by Christ and sanctified by the Holy Spirit.

But, on the other hand, the kingdom which Christ inaugurates and the Holy Spirit fulfils is *not of this world*. "This world", by rejecting and condemning Christ, has condemned itself; no one therefore can enter the kingdom without in a real sense dying to the world, i.e. rejecting it in its self-sufficiency, without putting all faith, hope and love in the "age to come", in the "day without evening" which will dawn at the end of time. "For you have died, and your life is hidden with Christ in God" (Col. 3:3). This means that although the church abides in the world, its real life is a constant expectation and anticipation of the world to come, a preparation for it, a passage into reality which in this world can be experienced only as future, as promise and token of things yet to come. The fruits of the Spirit (e.g. joy, peace, holiness, vision, knowledge) are real, but their reality is that of the joy which a traveller experiences when, at the end of a long journey, he finally sees the beautiful city where he is going – which, however, he has yet to enter. The church now reveals and truly bestows the kingdom, which is to come, and creation becomes new when it dies to itself as "this world" and becomes thirst and hunger for the consummation of all things in God.

The nature of the church is primarily to be understood as the Church of the Triune God. The Holy Trinity is the loving communion and source of the church's existence and, as such, the church is in the image and likeness of God. This being in the image of the blessed Trinity constitutes the mode of the church's existence, which, in fact, reveals her nature. Being in God, the church reflects God's unity in Trinity on earth. What is natural to God is given to the church by grace. The grace of the Trinity is the *starting point* for understanding the nature of the church, and especially for its unity in multiplicity, as the Holy Spirit shares one life and one being. The three distinct and unique Persons are one in life and in nature.

Similarly, the church exhibits a parallel multiplicity of persons in unity of life and being. The relation between God and the church is that, in the former, multiplicity or diversity in unity is the truth, whereas in the latter this is only a participation in the truth. In the language of the church fathers, the former is *ousia* (substance), while the latter is *metousia* (participation). The unity of the three divine persons in life and being is, therefore, the prototype of the unity of the church's persons in life and in being. As Christ himself says in his prayer for the church: "As you, Father, are in me, and I am in you, may they be in us, so that the world may believe that you have sent me." The mark of unity is collegiality and love, and not subordination.

Orthodox pneumatology or triadology, based on the "grace of the Trinity", supplies the basic ontological categories for Orthodox ecclesiology. The church is an icon of the Holy Trinity, a participation in God's grace. How does the church participate in God's mystery and grace? How is participation in the essence of God *metousia Theou* achieved? How does the church become an *icon* of the Holy Trinity? The answer, in its simplest form, is contained in the phrase "in and through Christ". Christ has established the bond between the image of the triune God and that which is made after the image, namely, the church, humankind. In Christ, we have both the *icon* and the *kat' icona*, "that which is according to the image".

Hence, we must say that the church is the church of the triune God *as the church of Christ*. The link between the Holy Trinity and Christology, that is, between theology and economy, demands a similar link in ecclesiology. The church is in the image of the Triune God and participates in the grace of the Trinity inasmuch as it is in Christ and partakes of his grace. The unity of persons in life and being cannot be achieved apart from this economy of Christ, and here we encounter what the New Testament calls the body of Christ.

Christ is in us, as we are in Christ

Christ is the head of the church, and the church is his body. It is from this Christological angle that we can better understand the multiplicity or diversity in unity which exists in the church. This attribute of the body of Christ is normally connected with the divine eucharist, because it is in the eucharist that the body is revealed and realized. In the divine eucharist, we encounter the whole Christ, the head, and the body, the church. However, the eucharist is celebrated in many places and among many different groups of people. Does this then mean that there are many bodies of Christ? This is not the case because there is one head, and one eucharistic body into which all the groups of people are incorporated in the different places. It is the Lord himself who is manifested in many places, as He gives his one body to all, so that in partaking of it they may all become one with him and with one another in the grace of Christ. In that there is one bread, the many are one body, for we all partake of the one bread. The many places and the many groups of people where the eucharistic body of Christ is revealed do not constitute an obstacle to its unity. Indeed, to partake of this body in one place is to be united with him who is not bound by place and, therefore, is mystically (or sacramentally) united with all. This is how St Athanasius explains the prayer of our Lord that the apostles may be one.

> … because I am thy Word, and I am also in them because of the body, and because of thee the salvation of men is perfected in me, therefore I ask that they may also become one, according to the body that is me and according to its perfection, that they, too, may become perfect having oneness with it, and having become one in it; that, as if all were carried by me, all may be one body and one spirit and may grow up into a perfect man.

St Athanasius concludes:

> For we, in partaking of the same, become one body, having the one Lord in ourselves. What is given in one specific place is something, which also transcends it, because of its particular perfection, that is, its being Christ's risen body.

The church is both in *statue patriae* and in *statue viae*. As "Christ in us", as the manifestation of the kingdom and the sacrament of the age to come, its life is already filled with God's grace of "joy and peace of the Holy Spirit", and it is this Paschal (Easter) joy that it expresses and receives in worship, in the holiness of its members, and in the communion of the saints. But at the same time as Christ dwells in us, in the church, "we are in Christ". We bear witness to this in our participation in pilgrimage and expectation as the people of God, and above everything else in the church's mission. For the church belongs both to this world and the world to come: it has entered the world to proclaim the joy to be found in Christ as well as the vision of a transfigured world and a redeemed creation. Accordingly the Orthodox Tradition, as the church of the saints, is, in fact, the church of the people of God and participates in the grace of Christ and the Holy Trinity.

The call to holiness binds them all into one church. Whatever one's position in the church on earth – clerical, ascetic or lay – it is the one body of Christ and the one grace of the Holy Trinity that remain the central focus. Each person is fully appreciated as a person in his relation to this one body and to the one common life and witness. Everyone is called to be a saint and, as such, to serve the mystery of Christ. Therefore, everyone, whatever his place or capacity, will equally be asked to give an account of his response to this calling on the day of judgement. Hence, Christians pray together for a Christian end to their lives, and a good apology before the judgement seat of Christ. The church is holy, or called to be holy, and this is an essential characteristic of Orthodox ecclesiology. It is the church of the triune God, the church of Christ, and the church of the fathers, the church of the saints, and the church of the people of God. It is the one, holy, catholic and apostolic church, in the personal, historical, theological and anthropological dimensions and unity, holiness, catholicity and apostolicity are celebrated in the whole mystery of the church. Orthodox ecclesiology is holistic and does not tolerate any arbitrary division between the one and the many. It is not tied to external uniformity or to pluriformity, but it is unity in multiplicity or diversity.

The one church is the continuation of the apostolic community of the first days. The churches are invited to overcome their present stage of stagnation or even of deadlock by being still divided, and there is need to restore their communion of unity in God's grace and love. They must find their common roots of their faith in the living Tradition, which is experienced and expressed in word and in the sacramental life of the one church. By the power and the action of the Holy Spirit, this communion must be realized anew in each period and time. The Church exists and is called to proclaim God's purpose for the world and to live it out in historical contexts and situations. The sacramental life is regarded as not coming from the gift of a special sacramental grace,[14] but from the working of the Holy Spirit, and the ideal presented is that of a mystical life in communion with God, lived in the church, which is the work of God's Spirit mediated through the sacraments.

The religious meaning of the sacramental life of the church is brought into connection with the incarnation of our Lord Jesus Christ. The sacraments are not the only means of grace, and therefore this sacramental life is not anything which denies God's free grace to humankind.

The mystery of the kingdom is to be announced today, and the unity of the church will be realized only with repentance, *metanoia*, humility and discernment, and with a return to our common sources. [15] The church bears witness to the truth not by reminiscence or from words of others, but from its own living, unceasing experience, from its catholic fullness. Therein lies that "tradition of truth" *(traditio veritatis)* about which St Irenaeus spoke. For him, it is connected with the "veritable unction of truth" *(charisma veritatis certum),* [16] and the "teaching of the apostles" was for him not so much an unchangeable example to be repeated or imitated, as it was an eternally living and inexhaustible source of life and inspiration. [17]

God's grace and purpose embraces all people. The whole Christian life is itself a matter of grace. In grace, from the beginning and according to the will of God, there acts invariably the unlimited goodness of the Father, the love of Christ that passes all understanding, and the inscrutable kindness of the Spirit. Everything in creation, providence and redemption, accomplished by the Triune God, through his good will, is a manifestation of grace. From an objective point of view, the whole world – and everything in the world – participates in God's grace and in the church it finally attains its reasonable and saving purpose. [18]

The church is called to discern by faith the signs of God's grace in action in history, in men and women also of other living faiths and commitments. Their meaning becomes clear only as they are understood in the perspective of Christ's coming. The church rejoices in these signs and recognizes them as a judgement and bearer of renewal for the church. In its search for unity it particularly needs to explore both what – out of its own experience – it may contribute to the overcoming of human barriers and divisions and also those insights which others may contribute to the life of the church itself. Is visible unity at all a possibility in this divided world? Nevertheless, God's promise stands. Christ prayed for the unity of his disciples, and it is on the basis of his prayer that the search for unity can be pursued with confidence and expectation that the aim will be realized in ever-new ways and with concrete results.

To reach this reality is the continuing struggle of the ecumenical movement. It is a joyful and gracious "cross" on a long way, a cross with obstacles and theological differences and differentiations, where God's grace and mercy embraces and fulfils the whole of humanity with energy, power, reconciliation and peace, and it offers only hope. It is this joyful and divine grace which unifies and liberates, mobilizes and sensitizes people's hearts and guides them towards a just world and God's kingdom. This grace is God's fulfilment of the salvation to the whole of humanity, and it offers to humankind as well as to the new creation the premises and the anticipation of the communion with the Creator. Unity surpasses the capacity of the human mind. All that reason can do is to understand it once it has been accomplished – but we cannot grasp beforehand how it would be accomplished: "The kingdom of God is not coming with things that can be observed" (Luke 17:20), but with God's grace and mercy.

The intense solidarity of Christianity with humanity, also shown with the people in need, in terms of economic and social issues, for example, can then bear fruit also in the political realm. It is significant that even Orthodox theology could open cracks in the monolith of authority and obedience. Further work on these perspectives needs to be done theologically. We are Christians who live in other times and contexts and with a new awareness of the social and political structures prevailing in today's world. We do not restrict ourselves to repeating what was said in the past in the socio-economic and political fields, but endeavour to produce a creative reconstruction or transformation of the world's assumptions and discoveries for a better future of humanity.

Do we still believe that the transforming power of God's grace is needed today in our world? Here, I would like to recall the prophetic words of the great theologian Fr Georges Florovsky that "everything in our life is recapitulated and identified in the self-emptying 'kenosis', the path of the cross". Our discovery of the value of the historical Jesus, in particular his active identification with the poor and the oppressed, ought to be integrated into the theology of the cross and of the kenosis of Jesus Christ.

A word about Christ's resurrection, where the cross finds its fulfilment, might be appropriate at this point. It cannot be dissociated from the cross; rather, the resurrection is given in the midst of the experience of it. To find hope within a hopeless situation, to have hope is an experience of the resurrection in the midst of the reality of the cross. Resurrection always happens in the midst of situations of evil, of alienation, of poverty, and of peoples suffering. Perhaps it may be appropriate to mention here an example from the Latin American situation. In the midst of terrible violence and a terrifying crisis imposed on the Latin American people, on the peoples of the so-called third world in general, by the financial interests of the great powers, international bankers – in the midst of this situation one can find the strength to mobilize, to gather together in solidarity. This surely constitutes a sign of new life and, as such, of the transforming power of God's grace.

We are currently living through one of the transforming moments in the history of worldwide religions. But there can be no doubt about the underlying realities – demographic and religious – which ensure that Christianity, in spite of being challenged or provoked today, sometimes even in a brutal way, will flourish in the new century and will play a specific and significant role on the world's agenda.

NOTES

[1] Cf. Philip Jenkins, *The Next Christendom: The Coming of Global Christianity*, London, Oxford UP, 2002, pp.1ff.
[2] Cf. J. Brosseder, "Grace", in *Dictionary of the Ecumenical Movement*, Nicholas Lossky et al. eds, WCC Publications, 2002, pp.497-502; J. de Baciocchi SM, "Grace", in *Catholisme Hier Aujourd'hui Demain*, vol. V, Paris, 1962, pp.135-72; C. Regan, "Grace", in *New Catholic Encyclopedia*, vol. VI, Catholic University of America, Washington DC, 1967, pp.638-85; M. Farantos, "Charis (grace)", in *The Religious and Moral Encyclopedia*, vol. XII, Athens, 1968, pp.78-85 (in Greek).
[3] Ch. Androutsos, *Symboliki*, Athens, 1930, pp.219-22 (in Greek).
[4] Ch. Christou, "Theological Studies", in *The Patriarchal Institute of Patristic Studies*, vol. 1, 1973, pp.236-37 (in Greek).

5 The term "grace" has been used with three main meanings. It may be the loving kindness of God shown in the redemption of humankind; the gift to humankind of a certain secret and mysterious quality conceived as coming from God apart from personal relationships; a state of grace – that is, the state of humankind that has come under the influence of divine grace or has received the gift of grace. Although there are certain passages in the New Testament which might be interpreted in accordance with these last two meanings, it seems clear that they do not arise from the exegesis of the New Testament, but have their origin in later thinking. As will be apparent, the origin of the term "grace" in a theological sense is entirely due to the New Testament and in the New Testament to a particular degree to St Paul. The meaning of the word "grace", as used in the New Testament, is not unlike its meaning as employed in common speech – with one important exception: in the Bible the word often represents that which is limitless, since it represents realities which are infinite and eternal. It is nothing less than the unlimited love of God expressing itself in measureless grace. Thus, in considering the Bible teaching on this great theme, equal attention should be given to all passages where either the term "grace" is used or the word "favour" is found. "Grace" means pure unrecompensed kindness and favour. What is done in grace, is done graciously. From this exact meaning there can be no departure; otherwise grace ceases to be grace. To arrive at the scope and force of the Bible doctrine of salvation by grace alone, we need to follow consistently the path indicated by the exact meaning of the word.

6 St John Chrysostom, *Homily in John*, XI,V.

7 *Oration 6:22*, in PG 35C, 749-572.

8 Cf. John Romanides, "The Filioque", in *Kleronomia*, vol. 7, no. 2, July 1975, p.299.

9 Cf. St Maximos the Confessor, in PG 91,1196B.

10 The Orthodox use of the apophatic method safeguards the true doctrine of God from that of mythology. This method negates all definitions and creative attributes of anthropomorphism, holding that the comprehension of God's incomprehensibility was the only safe knowledge about God. The Orthodox believe that God is beyond all human and logical categories and divine essence totally transcends knowledge and comprehension in this life and the next. Orthodox theology provides God's accessibility to human persons through the uncreated energies. God's relation to the world and to the human person is an immediate presence revealing himself to his people who praise and glorify his name. Like the physical sun, God in Trinity creates and sustains the world.

11 Cf. John D. Zizioulas (Metropolitan of Pergamon), *Being As Communion*, New York, St Vladimir's, 1985, p.41.

12 Cf. 1 John 4:16 : "God is love" points to the truth that God is Trinity.

13 Alexander Schmemann read a paper "Ecclesiological Notes" at the Institute for Contemporary Theology in Montreal, July 1965, which was published in *St Vladimir's Seminary Quarterly*, vol. 11, no. 1, 1967, pp.35-39.

14 It is difficult to define the Orthodox conception or teaching of "sacramental grace", since neither the Greek fathers nor the Orthodox church, by an ecumenical council or a local synod, have fixed a doctrine in all its details. A more systematic reflection of the question from the Orthodox side was not made before the 13th century (cf. The Monk Job 1270, and Michael Paleolog's confession to the synod of Lyon, 1274) and with more exactitude not before the 17th century. For this reason even the term "sacramental grace" is entirely unknown to the terminology used by the Orthodox, since the grace received through the sacraments is nothing "special", but simply the ordinary grace of God received through the sacraments.
   This late development of the sacramental doctrine, although mostly based on the holy scriptures and the holy Tradition of the church, is influenced in some of its details both by the Roman Catholic theology, as is surely the case with the Orthodox confessions of Peter Moghila (1642) and Patriarch Dositheus (1672), and also the Protestant theology, as the confession of Lucaris (1629, 1633) clearly shows. It is also true that with some exceptions the Greek fathers and Orthodox writers were mainly preoccupied with other very important matters to reflect and teach, but the relative parts of their writings mostly disregarded by contemporary Orthodox theologians, would give sufficient material for sketching a pretty full scheme of sacramental doctrine of the Tradition of the church more or less independently of the later Orthodox confessions and later or contemporary theological writings. Frank Gavin, in his excellent book *Some Aspects of Contemporary Greek Orthodox Thought* (1923, pp.269-393) – even if it was written sixty years ago – gives a perfect idea of what contemporary Greek theologians did teach and accept about the

sacraments, however without perceiving entirely its accordance with the older orthodox spirit of the church fathers.

[15] Cf. Mgr Basile Krivocheine ed., *"Syméon le Nouveau Théologien, Catéchèse I"*, in *Sources Chrétiennes*, no. 96, Paris, 1964, *Introduction*, pp. 39-40.

[16] St Irenaeus, *Adv. Haer., X*, 10,2; and *ibid.*, 26,2

[17] *What Kind of Unity?* Faith and Order Paper no. 69, WCC, pp.120-21.

[18] Cf. W.T. Whitley ed., "The Doctrine of Grace", in *The Theology of Grace. The Report of the Theological Committee Appointed by the Continuation Committee of the Faith and Order Movement to the Committee at High Leigh on 19 August 1931*, London, Student Christian Movement, 1932, pp.3-29.

"God, in Your Grace, Transform the World"

Biblical Reflection

REV. PROF. VASILE MIHOC

In modern thinking, world history was generally seen to be moving towards, or at least eagerly awaiting, the point where the industrial revolution and the philosophical Enlightenment would bring a new era of blessing for all. There was here an essentially eschatological story, still preached in our own days – from slightly different perspectives – by both capitalist and communist ideologies. This modernist dream of transforming the world only by our own will and efforts translated into theology, sustains a sort of Pelagianism, which can be summarized in the phrase: save yourself by your own efforts.

Modernity stands now condemned to building a new tower of Babel. Postmodernity claims that all this is just a power game, and therefore everything in this story is suspect. Unfortunately, the radical hermeneutic of suspicion that characterizes all of postmodernity is essentially nihilistic, denying the very possibility of the world to be enlightened, renewed, transformed.

The postmodern critique challenges us to pass judgement on the arrogance of modernity and, reflecting biblically and Christianly, to show again to the world how Jesus Christ is truly the way of the world's salvation.

As Orthodox, we have to reaffirm more strongly and with more clarity our theology of God-human synergy in transforming the world, founded in the theanthropic person and work of the incarnate Son of God, and to give our answer to modern Pelagianism by reaffirming the transforming power of God's grace in Christ, our Lord.

1. God – grace – transformation of the world. First of all, I think that we need to say something about the terms used in the assembly theme.

When we Christians speak of God, we mean the one and only true God. Many of the New Testament scholars of our day have problems in identifying the one true God, and related to this, in witnessing true biblical Christology. Some, having an overly lofty and detached view of God when they approach the Christological question, try to fit Jesus into this view; the result is a docetic Christ. On the opposite side, following the critical protest against this docetic view, a protest that started in the 18th century and continues to this day, historical scholarship tries to discover the "true Jesus" who, in its perspective, is not truly divine, the "historical Jesus" being totally different from the Christ of the church's faith. The god of this scholarship is a false god, not the triune God. Neither a docetic Christ nor the god imagined by deism or by liberal criticism would save or transform the world. There is no true knowledge of God outside Christ and his coming into the world as witnessed in the holy scriptures. "Who of men at all understood before his coming what God is?" asks the *Epistle to Diognetus* (ch. 8). [1]

Grace is also a term that needs clarification, given the erroneous definition it frequently receives. The Christian use of this term is based on its use in the New Testament. The term χάρις, outside the Pauline letters, is used only by Luke, in John 1:14-17, and rarely in the rest of New Testament writings. "In Paul, χάρις is a central concept that most clearly expresses his understanding of the salvation event... Naturally, the term does not have in every passage the specific sense of Paul's doctrine of grace... Specifically Pauline is the use of the word to expound the structure of the salvation event." [2] It means both the event of salvation and the "state" of those who are called into it; it is (God's) gift, operation and result of the operation at one and the same time. [3] It is actually another name for God's salvation of the world offered in Christ and made present to us by the Holy Spirit. We must say here that in many instances πνεῦμα is another New Testament word for "grace", therefore a synonym of χάρις.

The very important and meaningful concept of "grace" cannot be properly understood outside the Orthodox doctrine of the triune God. The Eastern Orthodox doctrine of grace, wonderfully formulated by St Gregory Palamas, who uses the concept of "divine energies" and speaks about grace as the uncreated energies of the triune God that penetrate and transform (deify) creation as fire penetrates iron, is the only understanding that corresponds to the truly biblical and Christian idea of our transformation (transfiguration) and the transformation of the world in Christ Jesus. Finally and essentially, grace is the glorified Christ who is offered, through the Holy Spirit, as God's gift (essentially the term χάρις means "gift") to his creation; or the glorified Christ who offers himself to be shared by us;[4] it is Christ's transfigured humanity as the grain of wheat of the new harvest (John 12:24), as the leaven which leavens the whole world (cf. Matt. 13:33).

Transformation, in the title, means not simply making the world a little better and the human a little more human. It also means us people becoming truly children of God and "partakers of the divine nature" (2 Pet. 1:4), and the world becoming the kingdom of God.

This eschatological transformation of the world is both present and future. God's grace, the gift of the Spirit, means, in the New Testament, both the realization of eschatology and a reaffirmation of it; so much is implied, for example, by St Paul's use of the term ἀρραβών, "guarantee" (2 Cor. 1:22; Eph. 1:14): the present possession of the Spirit means that part of the future glory is already attained, and equally that part still remains to be attained at the consummation, as fruit of our collaboration with God's grace.

2. The kingdom of God. There is wide agreement among New Testament scholars that the kingdom of God was central to Jesus' message. Two points are fundamental in Jesus' perspective on the approaching kingdom of God.

First, Jesus believed that God's purpose from the beginning was to address and deal with the problems within his creation through Israel. Israel was not just to be "an example" of a nation under God; Israel was to be the means through which the world would be saved.

Second, Jesus believed that this vocation would be accomplished through Israel's history reaching a great moment of climax, through which the creator God, the covenant God, would at last bring his love and justice, his mercy and truth, to bear upon the whole world, to bring renewal and healing to all creation. [5] In technical words, what we are talking about is election and eschatology: God's choice to be the means of saving the world; God's bringing of Israel's history to its moment of climax, through which justice and mercy would embrace not only Israel but also the whole world.

"Kingdom of God" or "kingdom of heaven" (mostly in the gospel according to St Matthew) in the Jewish mind was not a place in heaven where we enter after death. It refers to the rule of heaven, that is, of God, being brought to bear in the present world. In the Lord's prayer we ask that the will of the Father be done on earth as in heaven. Jesus' contemporaries knew that the creator God intended to bring justice and peace to his world here and now.

Announcing that the kingdom of God is at hand, Jesus, confronting some inconsistent dreams and visions of the kingdom of God shared by different Jewish groups of his day, goes back to Israel's scriptures and teaches – both in acts (miracles) and words – that the coming of God's kingdom implies transformation. God is not simply reinforcing Israel as she stood. He was doing what the prophets always warned: he was judging Israel for her idolatry and was simultaneously calling into being a new people, a renewed Israel, a returned-from-exile people of God.

As an example, the parable of the sower in Mark 4:1-20 and its parallels is not merely a simple illustration taken from the farming practices of Galilee. If we think of Jeremiah's (and other prophets') image of God's sowing his people again in their own land, or of Isaiah's metaphor of sowing and reaping as referring to the new creation that God will accomplish after the exile, we discover this parable as a typically Jewish story about the way in which the kingdom of God was coming. The quotation at the end of this parable of the text from Isaiah 6:9-10 (Mark 4:12; Matt. 13:14f.; Luke 8:10) indicates the true meaning of this "parable about the parables" (cf. Matt. 13:10ff.) which is the parable of the sower: in Jesus' own ministry, God calls into being a new people, a renewed Israel. Jesus is saying that the kingdom of God, the return from exile, the great climax of Israel's history – and actually the history of the whole world – is here.

Similarly, the parable of the Prodigal Son in Luke 15:11-32 is not only a general illustration of the timeless truth of God's forgiveness for the sinner, but also and foremost the story of eschatological return from exile, which was happening in and through Jesus' work. This was the good news, the εὐαγγέλιον.

On the same line, the sermon on the mount (Matt. 5-7) must be seen in the context of Jesus' announcement of the kingdom. The sermon ends with a coded but very sharp warning. The real new temple, the real house-on-the-rock, will consist of the community that builds its life upon Jesus' words. All other attempts to create a new Israel, a pure or revolutionary community, would be like building a house on sand.

Jesus has chosen the twelve – a deeply symbolic number, clearly indicating Christ's intention to reconstitute Israel around himself. This explains why the first commission of the twelve is restricted to Israel (Matt. 10:6,23, 15:24). The reconstitution of Israel will be the turning point in the history and life of the whole world (Rom. 15:8-9). Many Old Testament prophecies (e.g. Isa. 42) announce that Messiah, the King of the restored Israel, will bring justice and peace not merely to Israel but to the whole world. The gospels clearly say that when God finally does for Israel what he has promised, then the effects will ripple out to reach the whole world. Many, says Jesus, will come from east and west and sit down with the patriarchs in the kingdom of God (Matt. 8:11).

The last supper, the new-exodus feast, strongly points in the same direction. The Jewish passover was linking the feasters with the exodus, not merely by way of long-range memory but by constituting them again as the liberated people, the covenant people of Yahweh. "Celebrating passover at any time since the Babylonian exile would have the immediate and obvious meaning that the feasters were also celebrating, in faith and in hope, the real end of exile, the renewal of the covenant."[6] In celebrating the quasi-passover meal with the group of his twelve followers,[7] Jesus was deliberately evoking the whole exodus-tradition and indicating that the hope of Israel would now come true in and through his death and resurrection. The death-resurrection of Jesus is the central and climactic moment toward which had been moving the whole story of Yahweh's redemption of Israel. "Those who shared the meal with him were the people of the renewed covenant, the people who received 'the forgiveness of sins', that is, the end of exile. Grouped around him, they constituted the true eschatological Israel."[8]

3. The world in its post-Easter age. Jesus' cross, seen in the light of Easter, offers itself as the great turning point of history. It was the moment when the evil and pain of the whole world were heaped up into one place, there to be dealt with once and for all. If that is so, why, can we ask, do evil and pain still seem to be so rampant in the world? The early Christians were facing the same problem. The letter to the Colossians and Ephesians, in which St Paul celebrates the achievement of Jesus' cross and resurrection so magnificently, are written from prison, as the principalities and powers still have their way with him. This is a tension we have to live with. The victory of the cross is really working in the life of the world, but we also believe in the yet-to-come final consummation, when God will wipe away all tears from all eyes.

We live in the post-Easter age of the world's history. We Christians exist because of Jesus' resurrection. But this resurrection has its impact on the whole world, on the whole creation. Christ's resurrection means not only that Jesus is alive today and that there is life after death after all; it is also the death of death [9] and the resurrection of the world. This is clearly shown in the gospels by their stressing the fact that the day of the resurrection is the first day of the week.

Let us take as an example John 20:1 and 19. St John does not waste words. He knows very well what he is doing when he speaks twice on the first day of the week in relation to the risen Lord. It is not just that Easter day happened to be on a Sunday. "John wants his readers to figure out that Easter day is the first day of God's new creation. Easter day was the birthday of God's new world. On the sixth day of the week, the Friday, God finished all his work; the great shout of tetelestai, 'It is finished!' in John 19:30 looks all the way back to the sixth day in Genesis 1 when, creating human beings in his own image, God finished the initial work of creation. Now, says John (19:5), 'Behold the Man!' here on Good Friday is the truly human being." [10] St John then invites us to see the Saturday, the sabbath between Good Friday and Easter, in terms of the sabbath rest of God after creation was accomplished. There is a close parallel, in the gospels and also in the Orthodox liturgy, [11] between the seventh day when God rested in satisfaction over his creation and holy Saturday when the incarnated Son of God rests in the tomb after completing the work of new creation. [12] Then, on Easter morning. it is the first day of the week. It is the first day of the new creation. [13] It is the day of the kingdom of God. [14] Mary Magdalene, early in the morning, meets the risen Lord in the garden. She thinks he is the gardener, as in one important sense he indeed is: he is truly the new Adam – St Paul says: the "last [eschatos = eschatological] Adam" (1 Cor. 15:45). This is the new Genesis. The new world has burst into the old world, opening up totally new possibilities. [15]

On the first day of the week, Jesus came and stood in the midst of his disciples and said, "Peace be with you". This old Jewish message of shalom (peace) is here not just a standard greeting but deeply indicative again of the achievement of the cross, as St John at once indicates: "Saying this, Jesus showed them his hands and his side." With this comes the great commission (John 20:19-23), the word that stands at the head of all Christian witness, mission, all discipleship, all reshaping of our world. "Peace be with you," he said again; "as the Father sent me, so I send you." And he breathed on them as once, long ago, God breathed into the nostrils of Adam and Eve his own breath, his breath of life. "Receive the Holy Spirit." This anticipates the coming into the world of the Holy Spirit at Pentecost, which is the birthday of the church.

The church lives in the bright interval between Easter and the final great consummation. Christ's resurrection was the climactic event and fact of cosmic history. From there on everything is different. But the final great consummation is still to come. The final rest of God will take place only after he accomplishes, in the risen and glorified Lord, the reconciliation of all creation. [16] St Paul says that the creation itself will receive its exodus, will be set free from its slavery to corruption (Rom. 8:19-22), that death itself will be definitely defeated (1 Cor. 15:26) and that God will be all in all (1 Cor. 15:28). Revelation speaks of the final consummation in terms of new heaven and new earth.

4. The transformation of the world in Christ. Our living in this time after Easter and Pentecost is enlightened and empowered by the presence and work into the world, through his church, of the glorified Christ in the Holy Spirit. This is God's grace: the glorified Christ or the glorified humanity of Christ shared with humanity through the work of the Holy Spirit. By grace we are collaborators of God in the transfiguration of the world.

The gospels present us the narrative of Christ's transfiguration (μεταμόρφωσις). The story of the transfiguration of Jesus offers an example of perceptible change, Mark 9:2 = Matt 17:2: μετεμορφώθη ἔμπροσθεν αὐτῶν. The miracle of transfiguration of Christ clearly has an eschatological signification (cf. Rev. 1:14f.). What is promised to the righteous in the new aeon (cf. also 1 Cor. 15:51f.) happens already to Jesus in this world, not as one among many others, but as the inaugurator of the new creation. Before the eyes of his most intimate disciples the human appearance of Jesus was for a moment changed into that of a heavenly being in the transfigured world. This is the anticipation and guarantee of an eschatological reality. Jesus is manifested to the disciples as the Son of Man of the hope of final salvation (cf. the use in the gospels of ὁ υἱός τοῦ ἀνθρώπου, in connection with the prophecy in Dan. 7:13-14). They are to realize that the goal of his way through suffering and death (Mark 8:31) is the glory of the Consummator (Mark 8:38f. and par.).

The transformation of the world means first and principally our own transformation. St Paul speaks about the Christian as the "new man" and the "new creation". In the letters of St Paul the idea of transformation, in the two passages in which it occurs with the use of the verb μεταμορφόω (2 Cor. 3:18; Rom. 12:2), refers to an invisible process in Christians which takes place, or begins to take place, already during their life in this aeon. In 2 Corinthians 3:18 the apostle concludes his demonstration of the superiority of the new covenant (διαθήκη), whose gift and mark is the Spirit, by contrasting with the Jewish attitude (v. 13ff.: κάλυμμα, which conceals the δόξα) that of Christians: ἡμεῖς δέ πάντες ἀνακεκαλυμμένῳ προσώπῳ τήν δόξαν κυρίου κατοπτριζόμενοι τήν αὐτήν εἰκόνα μεταμορφούμεθα ἀπό δόξης εἰς δόξαν, καθάπερ ἀπό κυρίου πνεύματος – "But we all, with unveiled face, beholding as in a mirror the glory of the Lord, are being transformed into the same image from glory to glory, just as from the Lord, the Spirit." To Christians the Spirit has granted free vision of the heavenly glory of the Lord Christ. In this vision they undergo an unceasing and progressive change into the image of the one whose glory they see. It is the Lord himself, present and active by the Spirit, who brings about this change. St Paul obviously affirms that man cannot bring about the change only by his own activity; it is effectuated by Christ in Christians. By the Spirit the Christians see the δόξα of Christ. There is a mystical deification – say the Orthodox – that takes place through the grace of Christ, the Lord who is now fully spiritualized ("the Lord is the Spirit", says St Paul in the previous verse, 2 Cor. 3:17). The calling of Christians is to change themselves into the likeness of Christ (cf. Rom. 8:29).

For St Paul, the transformation of the world is a process by which the transcendent eschatological reality of salvation works determinatively in the earthly lives of Christians. St Paul surely shares the hope of the physical transformation of believers at the end of the days (1 Cor. 15:44ff., 51f.; Phil. 3:21). But he is also certain that the new aeon has already come with Christ. The Spirit, the ἀπαρχή and ἀρραβών of eschatological salvation, is already the possession of Christians. In virtue of the presence of the πνεῦμα, in whom the risen Lord is himself present (2 Cor. 3:17), the transformation begins already, and from within – though not only inwardly – refashions the Christians after the likeness of the

Lord, by giving them to share in the δόξα. There is still tension, however, between the "already" and the "not yet": ἀπό δόξης εἰς δόξαν "from glory to glory".

In Romans 12:2 the thought of transformation is changed from an indicative into an imperative and set in the sharp light of the doctrine of the two aeons: μή συσχηματίζεσθε τῷ αἰῶνι τούτῳ, ἀλλά μεταμορφοῦσθε τῇ ἀνακαινώσει τοῦ νοός, "Do not conform yourselves to this aeon, but be transformed by the renewing of the consciousness." Redeemed by Christ, Christians no longer stand in this aeon but in the coming aeon (Gal. 1:4). In conduct then, they must not follow the forms of life in this aeon, but the very different form of life in the coming aeon. But they cannot give themselves this form. They are changed into it on the basis of the renewing of their thinking and willing by the πνεῦμα. "Spirit" is used for "grace", which means the work of the Spirit in sharing Christ's salvation to the world.

The paradoxical μεταμορφοῦσθε which echoes Jesus' call for repentance (μετανοέω, μετάνοια) has in view the responsibility of Christians for the change becoming and remaining effective. Its concern is the new moral life in the Spirit as an obligation: "Become what you are." [17]

* * * * *

It was said that the book of Genesis "begins with a vast sweep of heaven and earth and ends with a solitary human body preserved in a casket in Egypt". [18] We can say that God's "Book" of the New Genesis begins with a solitary body in a tomb and will end with the all-glorious new heaven and earth. In between there is our working day, our time of synergetic action to the transformation of the world.

NOTES

[1] In A. Roberts and J. Donaldson eds, *Ante-Nicene Fathers*, vol. 1, Peabody MA, Hendrickson, 1885, 2nd printing 1995, p.28.

[2] H. Conzelmann, art. χάρις, etc., in Gerhard Kittel and Gerhard Friedrich eds, *The Theological Dictionary of the New Testament*, transl. G.W. Bromiley, Grand Rapids MI, Eerdmans, vol. IX, 1974, pp.393f.

[3] Conzelmann, χάρις, etc., p.395.

[4] The grace is both of Christ and of the Holy Spirit. Fr. Dumitru Staniloae writes that "the grace and all the gifts are nothing else than the bringing in us, through the Holy Spirit, of the goods present in our own nature divinized in Christ" (*Teologia Dogmatica Ortodoxa*, vol. 2, 3rd ed., Bucharest, Institutului Biblic si de Misiune al Bisericii Ortodoxe Române, 2003, p.316; and "The Spirit has not another role than to make our own the Christ's energies and the gifts that close us to his likeness" (*ibid.*).

[5] N.T. Wright, *The Challenge of Jesus: Rediscovering Who Jesus Was and Is*, Downers Grove IL, InterVarsity Press, 1999, p.35.

[6] Wright, *The Challenge*, 84.

[7] The last supper was not simply a Jewish passover meal. With regard to the calendar, it took place on the evening of Nissan 14, a day before the Jewish passover. This meal, which lacks the main characteristics of the Jewish paschal celebration, practically institutes a new Passover, the passover of Christ.

[8] Wright, *The Challenge*, p.85.

[9] Christ "has conquered death by death", as we sing at Easter in the Orthodox liturgy.

[10] Wright, *The Challenge*, p.175.

[11] For example, in the following hymn of holy Saturday: *"God blessed the seventh day./This is the blessed sabbath./This is the day of rest./On which the only begotten Son of God/rested from all his works./He kept the sabbath in the flesh,/through the dispensation of death./But on this day,/he returned again/through the resurrection. And has/granted us eternal life. For he alone/is good, the lover of man."*

[12] Fr A. Schmemann writes, "All Saturdays in the liturgical year receive their meaning from two decisive Saturdays: that of Lazarus's resurrection, which took place in this world and is the announcement and the assurance of the common resurrection; and that of the great and holy sabbath of Pascha, when death itself was transformed and became the 'Passover' into the new life of the new creation" (*Great Lent*, Crestwood NY, Saint Vladimir's Seminary, 1969, p.77).

[13] The first day of Christ's resurrection is also seen as the eighth day. Already the *Epistle of Barnabas* (ch. 15) considers this day, coming after the six (= six thousand years, for Barnabas, cf. Ps. 89/90:4; 2 Pet. 3:8) + one days of the old creation, as "the eighth day, that is, a beginning of another world" (in A. Roberts and J. Donaldson eds, *Ante-Nicene Fathers*, vol. 1, pp.146-47).

[14] The early church did not connect so much the Sunday with the idea of rest, Sunday being essentially for her the day of the Lord, the day of the kingdom, the day of eucharist. Fr A. Schmemann wrote, "For the early church the Lord's day was the joyful day of the kingdom. The Lord's day signified for her not the substitution of one form of reckoning time by another, the replacement of Saturday by Sunday, but a break into the 'New Aeon', a participation in a time that is by nature totally different" (*Introduction to the Divine Liturgy*, London, Faith Press, 1966, p.63). Thus, whereas the sabbath was primarily a day of rest, Sunday is primarily a day of joy and praise, of doxology and worship, of eucharist. Sunday is the day of our encounter with the risen and living Christ. It is indeed the day of the new creation, the day of the transfigured world, the day of the kingdom.

[15] On the same line, Earle E. Ellies observes that in St Luke the meal in Emmaus, on the evening of the same day of resurrection, is the eighth meal-scene in the gospel, where the last supper was the seventh (Luke 5:29, 7:36, 9:16, 10:39, 11:37, 14:1, 22:14, 24:3; probably the Zacchaeus story is not to be counted on this list): the week of the first creation is over, and Easter is the beginning of the new creation (*The Gospel of Luke*, Nashville and London, Nelson, 1966, ad loc.).

[16] If the sabbath is already fulfilled in the life, death and resurrection of Jesus, there is still another true sabbath of God, of which we read in Hebrews 4:9-11: it is the sabbath of the final, eternal rest of God and of his people, this sabbath that is still awaited in hope.

[17] J. Behm, art. μορφή, μεταμορφόω, etc., in Kittel, *The Theological Dictionary of the New Testament*, vol. IV, 1967, p.759.

[18] Clare Amos, "Genesis", in *Global Bible Commentary*, Nashville, Abingdon, 2004, p.1.

"God, in Your Grace, Transform Our Lives"

BISHOP NAREG ALEMEZIAN

The theme of the upcoming World Council of Churches ninth assembly (14-23 January 2006, Porto Alegre, Brazil) will be "God, in Your Grace, Transform the World". In this pre-assembly Orthodox meeting we are invited to discuss this theme in four sub-themes:

1. *"God, in your grace, transform our lives"* [faith, salvation, theosis];
2. *"God, in your grace, transform the church and the Churches"* [ecclesiology, unity, koinonia];
3. *"God, in your grace, transform our world"* [social issues, peace, justice, reconciliation, DOV, etc.];
4. *"God, in your grace, transform the whole creation"* [ecology and environmental issues and challenges].

I believe that these four sub-themes are coherent, interconnected and interdependent. Therefore, while they are treated separately and as complementary to each other, some overlaps may occur.

I will present the first sub-theme ("God, in your grace, transform our lives") as an exposition of an Armenian Orthodox perspective.

Introduction: *"God, in Your Grace, Transform Our Lives"*

"The biblical conception of human persons develops around a threefold thread: created in the image of God, fallen in sin, and redeemed in Jesus Christ."[1]

Humans, created in the image and likeness of God (Gen. 1:26-27), are in persistent search and longing for being in koinonia with their Creator. This calling and quest aim at the recovery of our lost image and likeness and reaffirm the very objective of our existence.

Sin cuts us off from God, fractures our authentic bond of love with God and our neighbour, and deteriorates the creature/s-creation-Creator intrinsic relationship. But since we are created to be restored in the *imago Dei* and because the only motive of God's creation of the cosmos is an act of love, God, through his mercy, cleanses, redeems and transforms us in the oikonomia of Christ (Rom. 3:23-26).

This love is directly and concretely manifested in God becoming the man Jesus, the new Adam (cf. 1 Cor. 15:22,45-49), incarnate by the Holy Spirit of the Virgin Mary and in sharing our humanity in all things but sin. Christ bore all the weight of human sin and offered himself on the cross as a sacrifice for our salvation. He redeemed us from our sin, reconciled us with God and offered us the gift of eternal life (Mark 10:45).

Therefore, this search, longing, calling and quest are clear indications that humans are theocentric beings created by a direct act of God initiated in the divine order of making male and female humans as co-workers to him (1 Cor. 3:9). Our origin, nature and purpose of existence make us beings dependent on God and belonging to God.

God's divine, unconditional and graceful love draws us to him (Rom. 5:15), because humans are not only created by God but they are created for God. Being in communion with God encompasses all kinds of relational realities, because in God we entirely find the purpose of our lives restored and transformed by his gracious presence (2 Pet. 1:3f.).

This restoration and transformation develops into a dynamic reality in God's gracious presence among us in Jesus. This grace is the "breath of life" identified with the Holy Spirit who caused the first man to be made in the *imago Dei* (Gen. 2:7). Additionally, this grace becomes a Christocentric incarnational[2] and sotereological[3] reality, enabling us to implore, "God, in your grace, transform our lives".

In the world of today, while relativism dominates and where God is put on the sidelines, this grace remains a gift of divine blessing (John 1:16). The Christian life rests on God's goodness and abundant loving-kindness showered upon us in blessing, as we pray during the holy eucharist: "For all good gifts and all perfect bounties have come from heaven, from you, who are the Father of light" (cf. James 1:17).[4] Thus, blessing flows from relationship of the Father, the Son and the Holy Spirit within God and us, humans, with God. At the heart of this blessing is a communion of love with God, into which we are invited in Christ and in the Holy Spirit (1 Cor. 1:9; Gal. 2:19b-20; Phil. 1:21; John 14.23; 1 Pet. 2:9; 1 John 1:3,6,7; 2 Cor. 13:13; Phil. 2.1).

This grace is a gift to be shared in the church, the community of divine generosity and communion for those who love and long for Christ.[5] All these make the church the body of Christ drawn into fellowship created by the Holy Spirit, where we live not for ourselves, not even for the proclamation of our Christian faith, but for God and the kingdom of God (Luke 22:30; John 18:36) through the life of God's grace, so that we become Christ-like beings and the everyday life of the church becomes an expression of God's love for the world. St Ignatius of Antioch in his *Letter to the Smyrnaens* writing about Christ and the church shares the following thought: "From whom we also derive our being, from his divinely blessed suffering, that He might set up a standard for all the ages, through his resurrection, to rally all his holy and faithful followers, whether among Jews or Gentiles, in the one body of his church."[6] This is how we render our Christian faith into daily life (2 Tim. 2:22), by living the gospel, the word of life, for the glory of God (John 17:5; 1 Cor. 6:20), as the people of God on a pilgrimage between the "already" and the "not yet".[7]

There is a genuine and indissoluble relationship between God and humanity. Human beings – the highest expression of God's creation on earth – have a vocation to glorify God with their whole life in obedience to God's commandments, reconciled with God in Christ, and by joining the Christian community and affirming its common faith[8] in gratitude for Christ's birth,[9] ministry, saving death, glorious resurrection and second coming.

Faith: human response to God's grace

Faith is unyielding trust on God. It signifies a personal relationship with God and the reception of the gift of our salvation (Matt. 15:28; Luke 17:19; John 5:24-26; 1 Cor. 12:3; 2 Tim 1:12). Through faith we believe that God exists and we trust his promises.

The object of faith is the whole revelation of God. Faith is conveyed through the holy Bible and Christian doctrine and liturgy, and is practised in the Christian daily life.[10] The apostle Paul says, "Faith is the realization of what is hoped for and evidence of things not seen. Because of it the ancients were well attested" (Heb. 11:1-2, NAB).[11] The affirmation of faith includes good works (James 2:17,26; Gal. 5:6; Phil. 2:12; 2 Cor. 9:8) and becomes a cooperative effort involving God's work (the gift of grace) and our work (the faithful response to it) over the span of a life-time.

In the church fathers virtuous Christian life is expressed by faith accompanied with good works:

- "The one who dies in his sin", Origen states, "does not really believe in Christ even if he says he does; if what he calls faith is not accompanied by works, it is dead."[12]
- "Do not rely upon the vain hope of the foolish, who say that the true faith alone is enough to save a Christian from suffering and to make him worthy of the kingdom. For as dead limbs are not of use for the activity of the body, so dead faith does not give strength to the soul."[13]

Faith is one of the three divine virtues with hope and love (Rom. 5:1-5; 1 Cor. 13:13) granted to the Christians by God to enable them to confess the Holy Trinity and live in communion with the Father, the Son and the Holy Spirit. According to St Gregory of Datev faith, hope and love are called divine virtues, because

> they are directed towards God. Through faith we see the supreme Good, through hope we wait for the supreme Good and through love we long for the upper Good. Also, through faith we are becoming able to receive God, through hope we are establishing communion with God and through love we are being united with God. Additionally, through God we are believing God, who only by his goodness and not out of any necessity created and redeemed us, through hope we are waiting for his promised mercy, because he is merciful and true and through love we are loving him, because he is Good in himself. For this reason we are loving our neighbour who is God's image and creature.[14]

Faith has a trinitarian basis, because we believe in the only true God who sent his Only-Begotten Son Jesus Christ and through him reconciled the world to himself (Mark 16:16; John 17:3; 1 John 5:1; 2 Cor. 5:19), and by the Holy Spirit brings new and eternal life to all who believe in Christ's saving mission (Rom. 4:22, 10:9-10; 1 Cor. 9:17; Eph. 3:2; Col. 1:25; 1 Tim. 1:4). [15] St Gregory the Illuminator confirms:

> The knowledge of the Father is the temple of his glory; those who enter it by confession of faith find him there. The wisdom of the Son is the altar of his birth; those who come in touch with him in the profession of orthodox faith he draws them closer to him and enables them to receive the Holy Spirit, the giver of all gifts and the divine light. [16]

Both in the Old Testament (cf. Heb. 11:1-40) and the New Testament (Matt. 9:23,28-29, 21:21-22; Mark 11:23, 16:16-18; Luke 7:7,9, 8:50, 17:5; John 11:25-27), faith in God has prominence and is expressed not merely as a personal attitude but as the confession and the proclamation of the church. Faith transforms the church to the living body of Christ manifested as a community of faith nourished by one faith and guided by one hope and vision. Because of this in the Orthodox church faith is confessed and enacted in the eucharistic community, holy eucharist being the core of sacramental life and the principal visible expression of ecclesial communion.

In the New Testament faith had a pivotal role in Jesus' ministry and in the teaching of the apostles, because faith in God operates in the Christian only in the context of the divine revelation and salvation in Christ (Mark 5:36; John 1:12, 3:15,18,36, 5:43, 6:29,40,47-51, 14:1; Acts 16:31; Rom. 3:22; Gal. 2:16,20; 1 John 5:9-10). For the apostle Paul faith is the necessary condition for participation in God's saving event effected through Jesus' death and resurrection (Rom. 1:16-17, 3:22,25-26,31, 4:1-25, 5:1, 10:9-10), offering the paschal reality of the Christian life as the gift of grace. Therefore, Christian faith is not an abstract concept or a dogmatic definition but it is the very person of Jesus Christ in whom we trust. The person and work of Christ are the object of our faith and the foundation of our trust. Constant usage of the terms "Christian faith" and "Christian faithful" preconditions Christianity as the religion of our faith in Christ – we are in Christ by faith (Heb. 12:2). [17]

The ground of our Orthodox koinonia in the triune God is founded on the common confession of the apostolic faith (2 Thess. 2:15) and manifested in the holy eucharist par excellence as the participation of the people of God in the body and blood of Christ (1 Cor. 10:16-17). Orthodox *lex orandi, lex credendi* reflects full doctrinal agreement and invites Christians to achieve full communion covenanting on the basis of *orthodoxia* and *orthopraxia* (1 Cor. 15:1-2), [18] because the church is genuinely expressed through the communion of truth and love.

The dogma of the church is based on the living Tradition inspired, sustained and guided by the Holy Spirit (John 14:26) in the revelation of God through the holy scriptures, the teachings of the apostles and the church fathers, the canons of the church councils and the liturgical and prayer life (Rom. 8:26) of the church. [19]

Faith, as the means of the transmission of all the promises of God to believers, is the foundation of the Christian spirituality and underlines the significance of the human response to God's grace in placing our whole life at the disposal of the gospel for the transformation of our selves and the world as the fulfilment of our Christian vocation.

Faith sustains Christian spirituality as the response of human beings to the revelation of God in our obedience to his will of accepting the divine gift of eternal and abundant life in Christ (John 4:14; 10:10) by the power of the Holy Spirit (1 Cor. 2:4, 6:17). Our living in Christ-likeness (2 Pet. 1:4) fulfils God's will (Rom. 12:2). Human beings share in the life of grace through the process of transformation and *theosis*, which remains a mysterious reality to be fully revealed in *parousia* (1 John 3:2).

Underlining the features of Armenian Orthodox spirituality vis-à-vis the Orthodox spirituality and the ecumenical spirituality, His Holiness Catholicos Aram I comments:

> In dealing with Armenian spirituality, it is important to bear in mind the following points: (a) Spirituality is more than contemplation or mysticism; it is an incarnational reality. (b) Spirituality is not confined to the institutional church and has not remained within ecclesial confines; it has always embraced the whole life of the people. (c) Liturgy occupies an important place in Armenian spiritual life. Liturgy is more than a church service. It is a living expression of our faith and hope, our suffering and vision, our values and perceptions, that make up Armenian Christian ethos. (d) The Armenian culture has been an efficient instrument of developing, shaping and expressing our spirituality. (e) The Armenian spirituality is simple, transparent and people-oriented…
>
> What contribution did the Orthodox churches make to the development of such spirituality? Let me pinpoint some characteristic features of the Orthodox contribution: (a) Spirituality is not only a personal matter; it deals with the whole community. (b) In addition to the word, the eucharist as well has a central place in spirituality. (c) The Bible and Tradition must be taken in their interrelatedness. (d) History is the place where spirituality takes place. Besides the text the context has a decisive role in shaping and expressing spirituality. (e) Spirituality is a holistic reality; it touches all aspects and dimensions of human life. (f) Spirituality also has a cosmic scope; it includes nature and the whole universe.
>
> Ecumenical spirituality, in its turn, has impacted Orthodox spirituality in the following way: (a) It reminded the Orthodox churches not to perceive spirituality only as going to the past, but also as opening to the Christ-event which is taking place here and now. (b) It challenged the Orthodox churches to move from self-contained to interactive spirituality, from triumphalistic spirituality to the spirituality of simplicity. [20]

Holy Spirit: the outpouring of grace

The Holy Spirit is the source of grace, transformation and sanctification (Lev. 19:2; 2 Cor. 3:18; 1 Pet. 1:10-16). The Holy Spirit constantly renews us in the image of God (Col. 3:9-10) and makes us "a new creation" (2 Cor. 5:17; Gal. 6:15; 1 Pet. 2:9) and "the temple of God" (1 Cor. 3:16). Through the Holy Spirit we are born again (John 3:3-7) and by adoption we become the children of God and household of faith (Rom. 8:1-17; Eph. 2:19; Gal. 4:4-7, 6:10; 1 John 3:1).

The connection of the Holy Spirit and grace is significant as *synergeia* between God's grace and our moral behaviour in relation to our salvation in Christ, which makes the doctrine of grace to intercede Christologically and pneumatologically. In the Armenian Orthodox church we pray to the Holy Spirit by the following words of St. Gregory of Nareg:

> Eternal and compassionate Spirit,… deliver us now from all unclean deeds that are not proper for those in whom you dwell, and may the shining light of your gifts not be extinguished within the reflective eyes of our understanding, for we have learned that you do unite with us in prayer and in commendable lives that are offered as incense. [21]

In salvation history the Holy Spirit transforms the sinners into a "community of saints" and enlivens the church as the fellowship of the Holy Spirit (2 Cor. 3:6).

As a trinitarian reality the Holy Spirit leads us to the Son and through the Son to the Father (John 3:34-35, 16:13-14, 17:3; Rom. 5.5). The outpouring of the grace of the Holy Spirit is the gift of the Father, the Son and the Holy Spirit.

Our Christian life is sustained by the grace of the Holy Spirit (1 Cor. 15:10; 2 Cor. 12:9-10). This state of grace is seen as a state of communion with God, a fellowship with the Holy Trinity, and a partaking of the divine. According to the hymns of the Armenian Orthodox church, the Holy Spirit is the vivifying and sanctifying "fountain of grace" [22] and "dispenser of grace and mercy". [23] Those who receive the gifts of the Holy Spirit are saved from "the dominance of Satan and become the sons and [daughters] of light [24] and inheritors of the kingdom," [25] and surrender themselves to the all-embracing grace originated in the active presence of the Holy Spirit.

Grace, the transforming and deifying presence of God, is revealed and poured out by the Holy Spirit (1 Thess. 1:6-8). [26] It is our "being in Christ" and a *koinonia* with God established through baptism – in dying with Christ and participating in the new life of his resurrection (Rom. 6:3f.; Col. 3:3f.) – and sustained by the holy eucharist. The *kenosis* of Christ Jesus (Phil. 2:6-11) enriches us in the church by the grace of the Holy Spirit (2 Cor. 8:9), which is an answer of our faith to our cooperation with God (Rom. 4:13-16; Eph. 2:5-8) [27] demonstrated in specific divine activities of the redemptive death of Christ (Rom. 3:21-25, 5:1-11; Heb. 2:9).

Charisms in the church are the gifts of the Holy Spirit and they are imparted to the faithful pre-eminently through the sacraments. [28] The church is a charismatic community sharing the gifts of the Holy Spirit, empowering its members to respond to God's call of adoption and to support God's mission in the world (Rom. 1:5, 5:1-11, 6:14, 12:3f.; 1 Cor. 1:4-9, 7:7, 12:4-5,7,11, 15:10; 2 Cor. 6:1; Eph. 3:2-10; 1 Thess. 1:5; 1 Tim. 4:14; 2 Tim. 1:6; Pet. 4:10).

The church lives in the continuous invocation of the Holy Spirit. This signifies God's transformative presence in the church. Through *epiclesis* the grace of

God purifies, renews,[29] revitalizes and transforms our lives. The primary context of *epiclesis* is the celebration of the holy eucharist and the actual consecration of the eucharistic gifts of the body and blood of Christ, inviting us to partake Christ, live in Christ, participate in the new covenant (Luke 22:19-20; cf. Jer. 31:31-36 and Isa. 53:10) and become the body of Christ in conformity with the will of God.[30] Epiclesis has an eschatological dimension, because the holy eucharist is the sacrament of the kingdom[31] and the eucharistic anamnesis of the mystery of Christ's death and resurrection is inseparable from his gift of salvation and his second coming.[32]

Salvation: God's gracious response to human sinfulness

Salvation is at the heart of the Christian faith as the entrusting of ourselves to Jesus Christ, the Son of God (Rom. 10:9; 1 John 5:5,13). God, out of his divine love, offers salvation to fallen creatures through his Son as the free and supreme gift of his grace (Eph. 1:7). Salvation is the result of God's initiative alone, who graciously, apart from any form of human merit, extends the invitation to all to receive his wonderful gift of forgiveness, transformed life and eternal hope.

According to St Gregory of Nareg (950-1003), a mystic saint of the Armenian Apostolic Church, God's saving grace will liberate us from the bondage of sin and through theosis make us partakers of divine energies:

A dew drop of your grace is exhilaration.
You give comfort.
You make us forget despair.
You lift away the gloom of grief.
You change the sighs of our heart into laughter.
Lord Christ, praised and worshipped with your Father
And exalted and proclaimed with the Holy Spirit,
Who alone became human like us for our sake,
So that you might make us like you for your sake,
Light unto all, merciful, almighty and heavenly in all ways.[33]

Through our acceptance of God's salvific work (Phil. 2:12-13) we become the recipients of God's reconciliation in awareness of the mercy and love of God (Rom. 5:10; 2 Cor. 5:17-21), restored in the divine life and communion that was broken by sin. Hence, salvation encompasses the deliverance of the individual from sin and acquires a communal aspect (Luke 4:18-19; Acts 2:38-47; Gal. 3:27-28; Eph. 2:19-22; Col. 1:18; 1 John 3:5,8). We, the assembly of the faithful, humbly acknowledge that human nature is distorted by sin and requires Christ's redemptive ministry to build us up as "living stones" (1 Pet. 2:5) and as a baptismal and eucharistic community.[34]

Our Saviour, Messiah and Lord (Luke 2:1; Heb. 5:9) assumed our human nature and humbled himself to be born as a man to bear our sins and to offer himself as a sacrifice for the expiation of our sins (Rom. 3:25; 1 Tim. 1:15, 2:4-5; Heb. 2:17, 9:14,26,28; 1 John 2:2, 4:10), to give his life as a ransom (Mark

10:45; 1 Tim. 2:6; 1 Pet. 1:18-19), to set us free from the power of the slavery of sin and death (John 8:32,36; Rom. 6:17-18; Gal. 5:1; Col. 1:13-14; Heb. 2:14-15; Rev. 21:4-7), to save us from the wrath of God (Rom. 5:9), and to justify (Rom. 3:23-26, 5:1, 9; Col. 2:13-14) and sanctify us (John 17:17,19; Rom. 1:6-7, 6:19-22; 1 Cor. 1:2,30; 2 Cor. 7:1; Eph. 4:24; 1 Thess. 4:3, 5:23; Heb. 10:10,14, 12:14).

God offers us salvation on the condition of our faith that Jesus Christ saves us from our sinfulness (Matt. 1:21; John 3:16; Acts 16:30-31; 1 John 2:2). Salvation is based on Jesus Christ alone (Acts 4:12) and forgiveness of sins is achieved by him through God's loving grace in the life-giving, renewing and sanctifying power of the Holy Spirit (Titus 3:5; Rom. 15:16; 2 Thess. 2:13; 1 Pet. 1:2; 1 Cor. 6:11). This divine purpose of salvation is the gift of God in Christ (Eph. 1:10; 3:9) and the covenant of grace between God and his people in the inauguration of the new transformed life of the believers.

In repentance we commit ourselves to the good news of God's kingdom (Mark 1:15; 2 Pet. 3:9), we ask for forgiveness (Acts 2:38; 1 John 1:9, 3:9) and cleansing of our heart (Acts 15:9) and conscience (Heb. 9:14), and we receive it by faith (Acts 16:30-31, 20:21, 26:18).[35]

The incarnation of Christ is culminated in his resurrection as the absolute means for restoring humans in their *imago Dei*. Consequently, incarnation is not only related to the beginning of Jesus' human life, but it is related to his earthly ministry and divine mission for salvation in taking upon himself our sins. Thus, it is the expression of the eternal love of the Father for all of his creatures in Christ's self-giving to death upon the cross for the destruction of death itself and restoration of our communion with the Father through the Son in the power of the Holy Spirit.

The doctrine of salvation intersects Christology, pneumatology, ecclesiology and eschatology.

Theosis: the climax of transformation

The ultimate vocation and supreme goal of humanity and creation is *theosis* (Col. 1:28, 3:11). Human beings are called by God to deification. To be in communion with God is accomplished through grace. By grace the Creator draws the creatures to him. According to the famous patristic saying, by the incarnation of Christ "God became man in order that man may become god" (St Athanasius, St Irenaeus, et al.).

Here are some quotations from the church fathers elaborating the understanding of *theosis*:

• "Among Christians, Ignatius of Antioch told his correspondents that they were 'God bearers' *(theophoroi)*, 'full of God' *(theou gemete)*. But it was left to Clement of Alexandria to give this doctrine adequate expression through the use of the terminology of deification: 'the Word of God became man in order that you may learn from man how man may become god'."[36]

- Athanasius, writing in his famous defence of the Trinity, *De Incarnatione*, said, "The Word was made man in order that we might be made divine. He displayed himself through a body, that we might receive knowledge of the invisible Father. He endured insult at the hands of man, that we might inherit immortality." [37]
- In his turn, reflecting upon the incarnation and coming of Jesus Christ, St Irenaeus has written: "Our Lord Jesus Christ became what we are that he might bring us to what He is himself". [38]
- "Therefore, as I have already said, He [Jesus Christ] caused human nature to cleave to and to become one with God. For unless man had overcome the enemy of humanity, the enemy would not have been legitimately vanquished. And again: unless it had been God who had freely given salvation, we could never have possessed it securely. And unless man had been joined to God, he could never have become a partaker of incorruptibility." [39]
- "For it was for this end that the Word of God was made man, and he who was the Son of God became the Son of Man, that man, having been taken into the Word, and receiving adoption, might become the son of God." [40]
- "The Lord 'conjoined himself with our nature in order that by its conjunction with the Godhead it might become divine, being exempted from death and rescued from the adverse tyranny. For his triumphal return from death inaugurated the triumphal return of the human race to life immortal'." [41]
- "Yesterday I was crucified with him; today I am glorified with him; yesterday I died with him; today I am quickened with him; yesterday I was buried with him; today I rise with him... We have become like Christ, for Christ became like us. We have become gods through him, for He became man for us." [42]
- "Christ humbled himself and became a man, the immortal became a mortal, in order to make all human beings partakers of his immortal divinity." [43]
- "Today (ref. to the feast of Epiphany) we are celebrating God's coming to human beings so we can go to God and be exalted. To put away the old man and put on the new man (cf. Eph 4:22-24), and just as in Adam we died, so too in Christ we shall live (cf. 1 Cor. 15:22)." [44]
- "But because we were unable to see the invisible or approach the unapproachable, [God] came and submitted to our humanity so that we may attain His Divinity." [45]
- "When will I be liberated from this temporal world, when will I be saved from this scandalous life? When will I join the assembly of angels and see your face my God?" [46]

Through *theosis* we are restored in the divine image and likeness, we are reconciled with God and out of God's loving purpose we receive the gift of salvation (Rom. 8:15; Gal. 4:6-7) [47] as his adopted sons and daughters. Through Christ's *theophany* we are deified in the sharing of the Father's gift of glory (John 1:14; 17:22-23). [48]

According to the *New Dictionary of Theology*,

[*theosis*] is the work of the Holy Spirit, who communicates to us the energies of God himself, so that we may become partakers of the divine nature (2 Pet. 1:4). The energies of God radiate from his essence and share its nature; but it must be understood that the deified person retains his personal identity and is not absorbed into the essence of God, which remains forever hidden from his eyes... Deification corresponds most closely to the Western understanding of the imitation of Christ... In this way we can fulfil what is seen as the biblical vision, that those redeemed by Christ will be like gods (cf. e.g. Ps. 82:6). [49]

A Christian becomes god by grace, but not God in essence. Thus, the distinction between Creator and creatures still continues. [50]

Deification is the gift of the Holy Spirit to make us Godlike in the participation of the new life in Christ. [51] It is the actuality of the divine life within the believer through the Holy Spirit. Sacraments are the special, visible and tangible means through which the transforming power of the Holy Spirit is transmitted to the believers as the grace of God and by the response of the believers is endowed on them as the process of sanctification enabling humans to participate in divine holiness. [52]

The mystery of our communion with the transcendent God becomes immanent in *theosis*, placing deification also within an eschatological framework through the operating presence of Jesus Christ and the Holy Spirit in the church and as our final being with God in the kingdom of heaven (Luke 10:20; 1 Cor. 13:12; 2 Cor. 5:1-4; Rev. 3:5, 20:12,15).

Ethical implications: God's grace in action in our lives

Christian ethics is relational and communal. It needs to be manifested in the reach out of the church for the transformation of human lives.

This fact mandates the church to become

- *a eucharistic body*, willing to share the life-giving bread and wine with a hungry world;
- *a missionary community*, sent to the world in the power of the Holy Spirit for the world's renewal in justice and freedom, and identified with the poor, the oppressed and the powerless in its commitment to struggle for justice, peace and human rights;
- *a doxological communion*, because by the decisions we make we give glory to God and proclaim the saving work of Christ (Rev. 5:12);
- *an eschatological reality*, making reconciliation tangibly operating among us as the dawning of God's kingdom through the ministry of the Holy Spirit and already beginning to reign in our present and preparing us to its fullness tomorrow. [53]

We actively and practically carry out this mission of bringing an unholy world to God through the ethical choices we make (1 Thess. 4:1f.; 1 Pet. 1:15) in a community bound together in a common faith and worship (John 4:23) and a fellowship of sharing and service as our response to the emerging political and social challenges. The genuine Christian faith is a practised faith in words and deeds – as witness and mission.

The Holy Spirit is the Spirit of communion in the distribution of grace in the church for the up-building of our fellowship with God (1 Cor. 12:7; Eph. 4:12; cf. Acts 2). Believers live by the Holy Spirit and serve God for the enrichment of the church's life and witness. This is expressed by our conduct as our lifelong formation in faith, our participation in the life of the community, our hearing and proclaiming the gospel, and our discipleship, mission and testimony.[54] Our behaviour reflects God's active presence, dynamic healing and graceful transformation in the midst of human brokenness in accordance with the values of God's kingdom.[55]

I would like to conclude my presentation with two quotations. The first one is a recollection of an excellent statement found in *BEM*:

> In the incarnation, life, death and resurrection of Jesus Christ, God has communicated effectively the mystery of the saving love to the world. Through the power of the Holy Spirit, the risen Christ continues this saving action of God by being present and active in our midst. For this purpose God continues to act through human persons, through their words, signs and actions together with elements of creation. Thus God communicates to the faithful, and through their witness to the world, his saving promise and grace. Those who receive in faith and trust this gracious action of God are thereby liberated from their captivity to sin and transformed in their lives. Those who receive this gift respond to it in thanksgiving and praise and are brought into a koinonia with the Holy Trinity and with each other and are sent to proclaim the gospel to the whole world. Through this divine action, communicated through words, signs and actions, this community, the church, is called, equipped and sent, empowered and guided by the Holy Spirit to witness to God's reconciling and re-creating love in a broken world. And so all who in faith long for fullness of life in Christ may experience the first fruits of God's kingdom – present and yet to be fully accomplished in a new heaven and earth.[56]

And the second one is a doxological affirmation from the sacrament of baptism of the Armenian Orthodox Church related to my sub-theme, "God, in your grace, transform our lives":

> O Lord God, great and glorified by all creatures, this your servant has bowed his/her head and has found refuge in your most powerful and holy name. Look with mercy, O Lord, upon this child, and by calling of your name expel and keep away the thoughts, the words, and the deeds, and all the deceptions of the evil one who is accustomed to deceive men and make them perish. Fill this child with your heavenly grace and grant him/her the joy to be named a Christian and make him/her worthy of baptism of the second birth of the holy font. And by receiving your Holy Spirit let him/her be body and member of your holy Church. And by leading a blameless Christian life in this world may he/she attain all good things of the world to come with the help of your saints, glorifying your unchangeable dominion. Now and forever and ever. Amen.[57]

NOTES

1   *What Christians Believe*, p.189.

2   "The essential theological approach of Orthodoxy consists in an uncompromising adherence to the confession of Jesus Christ as the incarnate Son of God, second person of the Holy Trinity. In this perspective, the incarnation is the most central event in history, the only true revolution, because in Jesus Christ and his redemptive work, the personal, triune God, the living God of Abraham, Isaac and Jacob, not only manifests but gives himself... to humanity" (Nicholas Lossky et al. eds, *Dictionary of the Ecumenical Movement*, WCC Publications, 2002, p.870).

3   "Contemporary theology must go beyond the notion of 'salvation history' in order to rediscover the meaning of the oikonomia. The economy of Christ cannot be reduced to its historical manifestation but indicates the fact that we are made participants in the... life of God himself. Hence the reference to eternity and to the work of the Holy Spirit." Michael Kinnamon and Brian E. Cope eds, *The Ecumenical Movement: An Anthology of Key Texts and Voices*, WCC Publications, 1997, p.402.

4   Fr Kourken Yaralian compiler, *The Sacred Music and the Divine Liturgy of the Armenian Apostolic Church*, New York, Armenian Prelacy, 1992, p.203.

5   The Orthodox generally relate the sacrament of baptism to the death and resurrection of Jesus Christ, and the sacrament of chrismation to the Pentecostal coming of the Holy Spirit.
   • "And they [Christians] confess the resurrection of Jesus, and the gift of the Holy Spirit which is intimately connected with it, as the foundation of the life and identity of the church, as the ground of hope for the whole world, and as God's pledge of eternal life." *Confessing the One Faith*, Faith and Order Paper no. 153, WCC Publications, 1991, p.67.

6   John R. Tyson, *Invitation to Christian Spirituality*, London, Oxford UP, 1999, p.56.

7   "The church is the instrument of the mystery of the salvation of the nations. It is the sign of God's love for all men. It is not over against the world, separate from it; it is part of the world. The church is the very breath of life for humanity, the image of the humanity to come, in virtue of the light it has received." *The Ecumenical Movement: An Anthology*, p.402.

8   The affirmation and profession of the common faith as the absolute truth are expressed through receiving, confessing and witnessing it (Rom. 10:10). St Athanasius writes, "The first kind of the comprehension of God is the profession of the true faith", while St Gregory the Illuminator says, "The truth of faith is a light for the eyes of the mind." Quoted in *Kantsasar*, in Armenian, the theological review of the Diocese of Artsakh, no. II, 1992, p.86.

9   God has revealed himself in Christ in a specific time and space. Orthodox theology makes a clear distinction between the inconceivable essence of God *(ousia)* and the energies of God *(energia)*. The latter, still being an inconceivable mystery, can be communicated through the Holy Spirit.

10 "According to *The Sayings of the Desert Fathers*, 'The old men used to say: God demands nothing from Christians except that they shall hearken to the holy scriptures, and carry into effect the things that are said in them'." Bishop Kallistos Ware, *The Orthodox Way*, Crestwood NW, St Vladimir's Seminary, 2002, p.109.

11 "Clement envisages the life of perfection as beginning with faith and ending with knowledge... The Christian life begins with faith, which is seen as the basis and origin of all knowledge (cf. esp. Str. ii. 2 and 4). By 'faith' Clement has in mind 'the conviction of things not seen' of Hebrews 11:1 rather than the more fiducial conception of Romans and Galatians. With the foundations provided by faith, itself indemonstrable, the house of knowledge may be erected." Cheslyn Jones, Geoffrey Wainwright, Edward Yarnold, SJ, eds, *The Study of Spirituality*, Oxford UP, 1986, p.113.

12 Thomas Spidlik, *The Spirituality of the Christian East*, Cistercian Publications, Kalamazoo, 1986, p.335.

13 Quoted in Michael B. Papazian's unpublished book "Light from Light: An Introduction to the History and Theology of the Armenian Church", pp.119-20.

14 Quoted in *Kantsasar*, in Armenian, the theological review of the diocese of Artsakh, no. VII, 2002, pp.39-40.

15 "The church confesses, worships and serves Jesus Christ as Lord. This confession rests upon a single central acknowledgment that in Jesus we encounter God as our Saviour." *Confessing the One Faith*, Faith and Order Paper no. 153, WCC Publications, 1991, p.43.

- "The message of the reconciliation accomplished in the death of Jesus is for all people the offer of liberation, through justification and the forgiveness of sins received in faith, as well as the gift of new life in the Holy Spirit" (*ibid.*, p.60).
- "The Holy Spirit descending upon the apostles the mystery of salvation..." (*The Rituals of the Armenian Apostolic Church*, Armenian Prelacy, New York, 1992, p.20).

[16] St Gregory the Illuminator, *Anthology of Sermons* (*Hajakhabadum* in Armenian), quoted in *Kantsasar*, no. 1, 1992, p.156.

[17] "The very term Christianity means to have the true profession of Christ. And only the one who has this true profession is called Christian" (St Athanasius; quoted in *Kantsasar*, no. 2, 1992, p.86.

[18] There is a deep relation between personal and/or collective experience of faith and the dogma upheld and taught by the church, as is stated in the following quotations:
- "Spirituality is lived dogma" (Spidlik, *The Spirituality of the Christian East*, p.37).
- In the matins of the Armenian Orthodox church we ask for Lord's mercy while we pray: "And again with one accord by our true and holy faith, let us beseech the Lord" (*Armenian Orthodox Church Book of Hours*, in Armenian, Armenian Catholicosate of Cilicia, Antelias-Lebanon, 1986, p.30).
- "If someone cannot understand the magnitude of the true faith, he/she cannot lead a life pleasant to God's will" (Evagrius of Pontius, *Kantsasar*, no. 1, 1992, p.154).
- "The profession of the faith of truth is the foundation and the root of all goodness. Our Lord proclaimed it the base of the church when he told Peter that he is a firm rock because of his confession of the faith" (St Gregory of Nareg, *ibid.*, p.154).
- "Orthodoxy has the light of true and perfect faith and sees clearly" (St Gregory of Datev, *ibid.*, p.155).

[19] "According to the bishop and martyr Irenaeus of Lyons, it is God's Spirit who keeps young and fresh the apostolic patrimony that was bequeathed to us once and for all" (Irenaeus of Lyons, *Adversus Haereses* III, 24, 1, *Sources chrétiennes*, n. 211, Paris, 1974, p.472), quoted in *L'Osservatore Romano*, N. 48 – 1 Dec. 2004, p.8).

[20] Aram I, *The Armenian Church Beyond the 1700th Anniversary*, Armenian Catholicosate of Cilicia, Antelias-Lebanon, 2002, pp.53-4.

[21] Very Rev. Daniel Findikyan, gen. ed., *Divine Liturgy of the Armenian Church*, New York, St Vartan Press, 2000, p.8.

[22] *Armenian Orthodox Church Hymns*, in Armenian, Armenian Catholicosate of Cilicia, Antelias-Lebanon, 1980, pp.521,523.

[23] *Ibid.*, p.236.

[24] Cf. Eph. 5.8.

[25] *Armenian Orthodox Church Book of Sacraments*, in Armenian, Constantinople, 1807, p.193.
In 451, the Armenians defended their Christian faith against the Zoroastrian Persians. When a group of priests were arrested and sentenced to death, with an exemplary courage of martyrs they encouraged each other, by saying: "By the power of the Holy Spirit we accomplished the tasks of our earthly lives. Now we are returning to our native world and household where apostles and saints are residing. We will become the members of the army of Christ, the Landlord and the Creator, who said 'Where I am, there also will my servant be' (John 12:26)" (Ghazar Parbetsi, History of Armenians, quoted in *The Teaching of Armenian Church Fathers*, in Armenian, Bishop Nerses Setian, Mekhitarian Press, Vienna, 1994, p.790).

[26] "Grace is the outpouring of the uncreated light descended on the rational and intelligible beings, and adorns them with the imitation of God in accordance with the conferred grace" (St Gregory of Datev, *Book of Questions*, in Armenian, St James Press, Jerusalem, 1993, p.140).

[27] "Grace is infinite. But it is finite according to the will of its distributor and the needs of its receiver" (*ibid.*, p.140).

[28] These quotations from the sacraments of the ordination of a priest, baptism and chrismation are clear expressions of the dynamics of grace:
- "The God-given, heavenly grace, which always answers the needs of serving the apostolic church, calls N. from diaconate to priesthood" (*Armenian Orthodox Church Book of Ordination*, in Armenian, Armenian Catholicosate of Cilicia, Antelias-Lebanon, 1958, p.36).

- "Blessing in the highest to the Holy Spirit that proceeded from the Father. The apostles drank from the immortal cup of graces and invited the earth to heaven" (*The Rituals of the Armenian Apostolic Church*, Armenian Prelacy, New York, 1992, p.37).
- "We beseech you, O Lord, to make this your servant worthy of your most precious grace whom you have called to the purification and enlightenment of the baptism" (*ibid.*, p.39).
- "Lord, Omnipotent God, Father of our Lord Jesus Christ, who granted the knowledge of your truth to all those who believe in you, and granted the power to become the sons and daughters of God through the rebirth from water and the Holy Spirit" (*ibid.*, p. 43).

[29] Here are two references from the hymns of the Armenian Orthodox Church depicting the Holy Spirit as the source of renewal:
- "The Renewer, who with his grace renews the cosmos and us from the sins of Adam" (*Armenian Orthodox Church Hymns*, in Armenian, Armenian Catholicosate of Cilicia, Antelias-Lebanon, 1980, p.93).
- "Today the heavenly were in joy because of the renewal of the earthly creatures; the Holy Spirit descended to the holy upper-room and by him the apostles were renewed" (*ibid.*, p.200).

[30] E.g. In the deacon's part of the holy eucharist of the Armenian Orthodox Church we read: "Let us beseech the Lord our God, who has accepted this sacrifice at his holy, heavenly and spiritual altar, that he may send down upon us, in return, the grace and the gifts of the Holy Spirit" (Fr Kourken Yaralian, compiler, *The Sacred Music and The Divine Liturgy of the Armenian Apostolic Church*, Armenian Prelacy, New York, 1992, p.191).

[31] "The risen Christ is exalted at the right hand of the Father, wielding the power of his kingdom. Although this will become apparent only at the time of his second coming, the church affirms it as a reality even now, hidden from our eyes, but nevertheless effective.
From the beginning of his earthly mission, Jesus proclaimed the kingdom of the Father (Mark 1:15). His ministry meant that the kingdom of the Father became a present reality among the people, 'in their midst' (Luke 17:21; cf. 11:20). Thus his own kingdom can never be anything other than to prepare and bring about the kingdom of the Father. This precisely is his kingdom: to persuade and lead everyone and everything into submission to the Father; just as the Son submits himself to the Father. Christ the king does not seek his own rule, but that of the Father, and therefore his kingdom 'will have no end'" (Lk 1:33) (*Confessing the One Faith*, Faith and Order Paper no. 153, WCC Publications, 1991, pp.71-72).
- In the holy eucharist of the Armenian Orthodox church, through the deacon we beseech: "Full of love and exceeding in the works of goodness we prayerfully stand at the holy table of God to obtain the grace of his mercy, when our Lord and Saviour Jesus Christ appears at his second coming" (*Armenian Orthodox Church Book of Hours*, in Armenian, Armenian Catholicosate of Cilicia, Antelias-Lebanon, 1986, p.702).

[32] "A 're-reading' of Christian traditions in the light of the statements of holy scripture brings all Christians together before God, who has made himself freely available to us once for all in Jesus Christ. This gift is laid hold of in faith through the Spirit, as we hope for the divine consummation which will be effected at the eschaton and is attested here and now in love – as the work of the grace of God" (*Dictionary of the Ecumenical Movement*, p.502).
- "There is a threefold experience of salvation, and Paul expresses this throughout his writings: salvation as past in our justification; salvation as present in the sanctifying power of the Spirit in our lives; and salvation as future expectation of the redemption of the body (i.e. resurrection) and participation in the coming manifestation of the kingdom of God (Rom. 8:18-25)" (*What Christians Believe*, p.297).
- We read the following in a thanksgiving hymn of the holy eucharist in the Armenian Orthodox church: "We thank you, Lord, for having fed us from your immortal table, by giving your body and blood for the salvation of the world and for the everlasting life of our souls" (Yaralian, *The Sacred Music and The Divine Liturgy*, p.201).

[33] Quoted in Papazian, "Light from Light", pp.119-120.

[34] In the Armenian Orthodox Church we pray: "The mystery of our salvation is awe-inspiring and marvelous. The one who was without beginning from the Father became a man from the Virgin. He endured the suffering on the cross and by his voluntary death he granted us the grace of living" (*Armenian Orthodox Church Book of Hours*, in Armenian, Armenian Catholicosate of Cilicia, Antelias-Lebanon, 1986, pp.433-34).

[35] The sacraments in general and the sacrament of penance in particular and liturgical circle of penitence and the whole dynamics of repentance are clear indications of repentance's paramount

importance in the life of the church. Some quotations from the hymns of penitence of the Armenian Orthodox Church confirm this reality:

• "Lord, as you have returned the publican to the knowledge of the truth, return me, the one gone astray, too, and have mercy on me" (p.163);

• "I presented my sins to you, Christ, because you are the physician of souls and the Lord of lives; heal also my infirmities, since you only are merciful" (p.168);

• "I beseech you, Lord, accord me the possibility of washing away my sins through repentance" (p.183);

• "All-sufficient grace of mercy, on the awesome day grant me pardon and save me" (p.199);

• "Save me, God, from my multiple sins and make me worthy of your holy kingdom; have mercy on me" (p.208).

(All quoted from *Armenian Orthodox Church Hymns*, in Armenian, Armenian Catholicosate of Cilicia, Antelias-Lebanon, 1997).

36 Spidlik, *The Spirituality of the Christian East*, p.46.

37 *What Christians Believe*, p.303.

38 John R. Tyson, *Invitation to Christian Spirituality*, Oxford UP, 1999, p.8.

39 St Irenaeus, in *ibid.*, p.66.

40 Spidlik, *The Spirituality of the Christian East*, p.351.

41 St Gregory of Nyssa, quoted in J.N.D. Kelly, *Early Christian Doctrines*, Harper & Row, 1960, pp.381-82.

42 St Gregory of Nazianzus, in Spidlik, *The Spirituality of the Christian East*, p.34

43 St Gregory the Illuminator, quoted in St Gregory of Datev, *Vosgeporig*, in Armenian, Yerevan, 1995, p.150.

44 St Gregory the Theologian, *ibid.*, p.151.

45 *Eghishe, History of Vardan and the Armenian War*, transl. Robert M. Thomson, quoted in Papazian, "Light from Light", p.75.

46 St Nerses of Lampron, in Armenian, quoted in a church Sunday bulletin.

47 "The Greek fathers understood this to mean that at the fall humanity lost the likeness but retained the image, so that the Christian life is best conceived as the restoration of the lost likeness to those who have been redeemed in Christ." Sinclair B. Ferguson, David E. Wright, J.I. Packer eds, *New Dictionary of Theology*, InterVarsity Press, 1988, p.189.

48 The Father is the ground of *theosis*: "The Father creates man through the Son and sanctifies him in the Spirit; man gives glory to the Father through the Son in the Holy Spirit. This is the 'royal highway' of human deification. St Basil wrote: 'Thus the way of the knowledge of God lies in the One Spirit through the One Son to the One Father, and conversely, natural goodness, inherent holiness, and royal dignity extend from the Father through the Only-begotten to the Spirit'" Spidlik, *The Spirituality of the Christian East*, pp. 44-45).

• "From Origen the Eastern spiritual writers learned that the deification of the Christian is his participation in the glory of Christ; it culminates in an experience analogous to that of the apostles on Tabor, an experience which corresponds to the highest form of the spiritual exegesis of scripture" (*ibid.*, p.342).

• "The vision of light is the vision of God himself; of God, however, in his energies and not in his essence. What the saints see is the same uncreated light that shone from Christ at the transfiguration on Mount Tabor, and that will shine from him equally at his second coming" (Jones et al., *The Study of Spirituality*, pp.251-52).

49 *New Dictionary of Theology*, p.189.
"The first clearly articulated concept of the application of the work of Christ to the sinful human condition is developed in the East in connection with the Christus Victor view of the work of Christ. This view is known as theosis or deification" (*What Christians Believe*, p.303).

50 The distinction between God's essence and energies is indicated in the following quotations:

• "...the essence-energies distinction is a way of stating simultaneously that the *whole* God is inaccessible, and that ... God in his outgoing love has rendered himself accessible to man. By virtue of this distinction between the divine essence and the divine energies, we are able to affirm the possibility of a direct or mystical union between man and God – what the Greek fathers term the *theosis* of man, his 'deification' – but at the same time we exclude any pantheistic identification between the two; for man participates in the energies of God, not in the essence" (Bishop Kallistos Ware, *The Orthodox Way*, pp.22-23).

• "Lossky believed that in the spiritual life of the Eastern church, 'The way of the imitation of Christ is never practised... Indeed, this way seems to have a certain lack of fullness; it would seem to imply a somewhat external attitude towards Christ'. Eastern spirituality 'may instead be defined as a *life in Christ*'" (Spidlik, *The Spirituality of the Christian East*, p.39).

• "He [Gregory Palamas] draws a distinction between the essence or inner being of God and his energies or acts of power. The essence indicates the divine transcendence and otherness; and as such it remains unknowable not only in the present life but in the age to come, not only to humankind but to the angels – it is *radically* unknowable... But, unknowable in his essence, God is dynamically disclosed to us in his energies, which permeate the universe and in which we humans can directly participate, even in this present life. These energies are not an intermediary between God and man, but the living God himself in action; and so, sharing in the divine energies, the saints are indeed enjoying the true vision of God 'face to face'" (Jones et al., *The Study of Spirituality*, pp. 250-51).

• "Athanasius, even though he clearly identified sonship and deification, took great care to note that this assimilation was not identification: it does not make us 'as the true God or his word, but as it has pleased God who has given us that grace'" (*ibid.*, p.46). cf. Eph. 5:1-2; referring to the imitation of Christ.

[51] In the Hymn of Vesting of the holy eucharist of the Armenian Orthodox Church we read: "Through the passion of your Only-Begotten Son all creatures came to life anew, and humans made immortal, adorned in inviolate garments" (Yaralian, *The Sacred Music and The Divine Liturgy*, p.143). This understanding of the formula 'in Christ' has been used in the New Testament approximately 165 times.

[52] "As is very hard for the creatures of water to live on land and the creatures of land to live in water, it is much harder for humans to receive the gifts of the Holy Spirit without faith" (St Yeghishe, *Kantsasar*, no. 1, 1992, p.63).

• "The goal of the spiritual life is, for Maximus, deification *(theösis)*, and the foundation of this is laid for all Christians in their baptism: Baptized in Christ through the Spirit, we receive the first incorruption according to the flesh. Keeping this original incorruption spotless by giving ourselves to good works and by dying to our own will, we await the final incorruption bestowed by Christ in the Spirit" (Jones et al., *The Study of Spirituality*, p.194).

[53] "Faith alone remains the crucial condition of participating in this secure promise. And where faith is weak, grace continues to awaken and sustain it. The Holy Spirit is determined to prevail over idolatry and disbelief in God's own time. But this assurance is not to be held in such a way as to diminish faithful good works or neglect the responsibilities of human freedom." Thomas C. Oden, *The Rebirth of Orthodoxy*, San Francisco, Harper, 2003, p.44.

[54] In a prayer from the night hour prayer of the Armenian Orthodox Church, we ask God: "Receive now our supplications and make us to remain in the orthodox faith and virtuous conduct." *The Teaching of Armenian Church Fathers*, in Armenian, Bishop Nerses Setian, Mekhitarian Press, Vienna, 1994, p.652.

[55] "Several attempts have been made to define that aspect in our nature which makes us capable of being transformed by God's grace. Perhaps one can recognize it in two human capacities. The first is our ability to make moral choices; in such decisions, when we reach for the highest good we know, God is leading us on to himself, whether we recognize the fact or not. The second is our ability to know and love other human beings. God does not allow our love to stop there, but enables it to reach through the other human being to himself. This is one way in which the second great commandment, to love our neighbour, is 'like' the first commandment, to love God (Matt. 22:37-39). Whenever we act as responsible, loving persons, we are in the field of grace, and exercising our spiritual priesthood" (Jones et al., *The Study of Spirituality*, pp.12-13).

[56] *Baptism, Eucharist and Ministry, 1982-1990: Report on the Process and Responses*, WCC Publications, 1990, pp.143-4. Quoted in *Dictionary of the Ecumenical Movement*, p.1005.

[57] *The Rituals of the Armenian Apostolic Church*, New York, Armenian Prelacy, 1992, p.23.

"God, in Your Grace, Transform the Church and the Churches"

Ecclesiology, Unity, Koinonia

REV. PROF. DR VIOREL IONITA

A substantial approach to the second sub-theme of our meeting "God, in your grace transform the church and the churches" through an ecclesiological perspective focusing on unity and koinonia is an enterprise beyond our possibilities given the frame of this meeting. Therefore, I will simply offer some comments as input for our discussion. I will start by commenting on the concepts of "transforming the church and the churches" as well as on the concepts of koinonia and of church unity and then formulate some final remarks for further discussion.

The theme for the next WCC Assembly: "God, in Your Grace, Transform the World" is primarily an invocation, which may indicate that the organizers of this assembly expect a complex approach mainly through prayers and meditations. From an Orthodox point of view we hope that the theological and pneumatological dimension of this theme will be fully taken into consideration. On the other hand, for us, this theme sounds somehow incomplete and open to different possible interpretations. Therefore, we have to be clear from the beginning that we ask God to transform the world according to his divine will, and not simply according to different political or economic expectations of this world.

As Metropolitan Gennadios of Sassima underlined in a recent study:

> Power, happiness, peace, achievement, bliss are conditional upon open-hearted receptivity towards God through the self-surrender of faith. Through the generous love or gift of God in grace, salvation is bestowed and a new world of blessings is opening. A world transformed to a new reality. Man is saved, not by anything proceeding from himself or from his own nature. Salvation proceeds from God and is exhibited in the cross of Christ. [1]

The invocation to God to transform the church and the churches as formulated in our sub-theme is a rather provocative formulation. Why one church on one side and many churches on the other side? Which church is in singular opposite or parallel to the other churches? This formulation reminds us of the remark in the final report of the Special Commission on Orthodox Participation in the WCC which identified "two basic ecclesiological self-understandings, namely of those churches (such as the Orthodox) which identify themselves with the one, holy, catholic and apostolic church, and those which see themselves as parts of the one, holy, catholic and apostolic church". In the Faith and Order Paper on

"The Nature and Purpose of the Church" the same idea is expressed as follows: "Churches understand their relation to the one, holy, catholic and apostolic church in different ways. This has a bearing upon the way they relate to other churches and their perception of the road to visible unity."[2] In any case the invocation to God to transform either one church or many churches or even all churches together refers actually to the relationship between God, the Holy Spirit, and the church or the churches, respectively.

For Dumitru Staniloae, the church "is participation in the mystery of the cross and resurrection in the power of the Holy Spirit".[3] The Holy Spirit continues the revelation of Christ

> through the act of bringing the church into existence, and through the practical organization of her structures, that is, through the initial putting of them into practice. It is the same Spirit who afterwards maintains the church as a permanent milieu for the effective power of revelation once this has been brought to a close in Christ, or rather perfected as both content and way of being put into practice. Thus, the Holy Spirit keeps the church true to the revelation closed in Christ, and to scripture and tradition which make Christ present and communicate him.

The Holy Spirit maintains these three, that means church, scripture and Tradition, as parts and aspects of the same integral unity.[4]

The Holy Spirit, the Paraclete promised by Christ, is the true centre of the church's life, from baptism and confirmation to holy communion, to priestly ordination, marriage, anointing of the sick, and confession, in which the charismatic element can clearly be recognized. In this way, the dualism between the "institutional" and the "charismatic" can be overcome, when we accept that Christology must not be separated from pneumatology. "In the Spirit, the institutional becomes charismatic and the charismatic becomes institutional", says Metropolitan John of Pergamon, referring to the well-known formulation of St Irenaeus: *Ubi ecclesia ibi est spiritus Dei, et ubi spiritus Dei, illic ecclesia.*[5]

In this respect the church cannot be separated from the Holy Spirit; the Spirit is not external to the church. André Scrima underlined that the church has been founded by God and belongs to God.[6] Without the Holy Spirit the church cannot be church any more; it is the Holy Spirit who keeps the church alive. Along these considerations one can ask what the invocation to God to transform the church may mean. The idea of transforming the church reminds us of the concept launched by the Groupe des Dombes about the conversion of the churches.

Although the book *For the Conversion of the Churches* published in 1991 in its original French version "is addressed to the Roman Catholic and Protestant churches in order to invite them to converge in converting together to the Lord",[7] even if it sometimes mentions also the Orthodox, the concept of the conversion of the churches has been used in larger ecumenical circles. Starting from the biblical term of metanoia, "which combines the ideas of repentance and conversion", the Groupe des Dombes stressed "that the unity as Christ wishes and by the means which he desires must pass by way of conversion of the churches, just where they feel themselves strongest and most assured in their conviction".[8]

The idea of churches' conversion to unity needs to be clarified in terms of the relationship between the church and her own unity; as if unity were something external to the church, in other words, how the churches relate themselves to that unity. Unity is not in front of the churches or above them, but rather something essential, which belongs to the essence, to the very being of the church. If the unity of the church has been destroyed through schisms and separation, in this case, unity is somehow behind the divided churches and not in front of them. Furthermore the churches cannot turn back to their unity simply through conversion or repentance for their historical mistakes without overcoming the doctrinal aspects of their division.

The Groupe des Dombes identified the following three aspects of conversion: (1) Christian conversion, (2) ecclesial conversion, and (3) confessional conversion. In the end, for this group,

> all conversions go through the stage of confessing guilt. Our confessions have to "make confession", to move forward to admitting their limitations and inadequacies, even sins. Each confessional family has to acknowledge that there are elements of Christian tradition which it is incapable, at least for the moment, of receiving and incorporating into its own existence.[9]

We appreciate the ecumenical effort of the Groupe des Dombes to find new ways for bringing closer the two occidental churches, as well as for bringing into the ecumenical scene the idea of conversion from sin to Jesus Christ and taking him as reference for all ecumenical effort. We have some difficulties with the understanding of the church in this context, which is considered almost exclusively in her human dimension, which is expressed more evidently in the perception of the church as sinner.

The question whether the church can sin or not is actually central for the understanding of the church in her theandric (divine and human) character. As the mystical body of Christ, the church has as her head the Lord himself under the guidance of the Holy Spirit and in this respect the church cannot sin. On the other hand, if we say that the members of the church are sinners either as individuals or as groups, we have to be careful not to separate completely the sinner members form the holy body. In order to avoid such a separation we have to remember that the holiness of the church is a gift of God to human beings, who confess their sins in every worship service, and the sins are forgiven by the Father in Christ's name by the power of the Holy Spirit. In this respect the church is not a simple community of sinners, but a community of human beings whose sins have been forgiven. We should not forget that confession of sins is a sacrament (mysterion) in Orthodox theology.

The Faith and Order Paper on "The Nature and Purpose of the Church" also approaches the issue of "church and sin". The different views on that matter are presented in a box and not in the main text in the form of "for some" and "others" without specific indication so that each one could recognize his or her view. The Orthodox will recognize themselves in the following presentation: "For some it is impossible to say 'the church sins' because they see the church as a gift of God, and as such marked by God's holiness. The church is the spotless Bride of

Christ (Eph. 5:25-27); it is the children of God who received God's incarnate Word through faith; it is the holy people of God, 'justified by the faith of Christ'; as such, the church cannot sin, 'lest Christ be the minister of sin' (Gal. 2:17). This gift of the church is lived out in fragile human beings who are liable to sin, but the sin of the members of the church are not sins of the church. The church is rather the locus of salvation and healing, and not the subject of sin."[10] There are also opinions of "others" that the church does sin "because they define the church as the communion of its members, who at the same time as being believers created by the Spirit and Christ's own body, in this world are still sinful beings". We regret that these different opinions are exposed in this paper one after the other without any comment or intention to bring them into a dialogue. To simply do justice to every doctrinal view is not necessarily the best ecumenical way.

Coming back to the concept of the conversion of churches we consider that it will be more appropriate to speak about conversion of people or even of Christians, as about the conversion of churches. In this sense we agree completely with the Groupe des Dombes that "conversion can take on very diverse forms: a sudden intervention of something new and unheard-of, a slow and continuous progression, the crossing of a series of thresholds. It directly concerns the personality of each believer who is becoming what he or she already is",[11] under the inspiration of the Holy Spirit.

Another concept in the sub-theme for our discussion here is koinonia, which has been brought into the ecumenical discussion by Orthodox contributions. The Ecumenical Patriarchate's encyclical of 1920, which was addressed to "all churches of Christ in every place", thus also to the non-Orthodox churches, has already made an initial proposal for the founding of a "federation of churches", a *koinonia ton ekklesion*, despite the existing differences in dogma.[12] Obviously the term koinonia was used here in a broader sense without its ecclesiological and eucharistic connotations.

At the fifth world conference of the WCC Faith and Order Commission (Santiago de Compostela, Spain, August 1993) koinonia was one of the main items of discussion. The final message of that conference speaks about "the koinonia we seek and which we have experienced"; "this koinonia which we share"; "the koinonia we experience" as well as about "the deeper koinonia which is our goal" and which "will be a sign of hope for all". We notice here a very variable understanding of koinonia; which on the one hand the churches are seeking, and on the other hand they have already experienced.

The Faith and Order paper "The Nature and Purpose of the Church" underlines that

> the notion of koinonia (communion) has become fundamental for revitalizing a common understanding of the nature of the church and its visible unity. The term koinonia (communion, participation) is used in the New Testament, patristic and Reformation writings in relation to the church. Although in later centuries the term remained in use, it is being reclaimed today in the ecumenical movement as a key to understanding the nature and the purpose of the church. Due to its richness of mean-

ing, it is also a convenient notion for assessing the degree of communion in various forms already achieved among Christians within the ecumenical movement. [13]

We fully agree with the message from Santiago de Compostela when it underlines that in the New Testament

the basic verbal form from which the noun koinonia derives means "to have something in common", "to share", "to participate", "to have part in", "to act together" or "to be in a contractual relationship involving obligations of mutual accountability". The word koinonia appears in key situations, for example, the reconciliation of Paul with Peter, James and John (Gal. 2:9), the collection for the poor (Rom. 15:26; 2 Cor. 8:4), the experience and witness of the church (Acts 2:42-45).

We have to accept that today the term koinonia is used for everything and so in danger of losing its original meaning. In the end it is important how we really understand that notion for the relationship between the churches today, or even between the different churches within the WCC. Metropolitan John of Pergamon, noticing already some years ago that "the concept of koinonia is gaining ground in the agenda of the WCC, and this is a good thing", underlined that

it is in any case important to underline the critical significance of this concept for the ecumenical movement. Orthodox ecclesiology will have to make a crucial contribution on this matter, on which I personally believe the future of the ecumenical movement will depend a great deal. [14]

The churches in the Dialogue Commission of the Conference of European Churches organized a meeting with some European members of the WCC Commission on Faith and Order in Armenia (June 2001), where they discussed the Faith and Order text on "The Nature and Purpose of the Church", and recognized

the many ways in which the term 'koinonia' has been a positive tool in the ecumenical task. In bringing together many insights from different traditions it has helped us to understand one another and, more importantly, our faith. It has a background in the Bible. It describes the communion, established through Christ, of the human person with God, with his or her neighbour, and the integrity within the human person. In embracing terms like communion, fellowship and community, and yet being more than any one of these, it has been profoundly illuminating. However, we have some caution about its use.

At that meeting in Armenia some critical remarks were made in relation to the term koinonia, which "may become a barrier to unity by smothering real differences, or because those from some traditions will claim that they are the ones who own the best interpretation". It was even recommended that

we need to beware of using terms, which only a few may be able to understand fully. There are risks in using words from languages no longer in common use, because they seem to suggest an authority, which may not be there. We need to accept the challenge to express our faith in vernacular languages or in a "lingua franca". Christianity must be expressed within the specificity of our own cultures. [15]

These comments underline that at least some theologians are no longer happy with the way the concept of koinonia is interpreted or even misinterpreted. According to Orthodox understanding, koinonia describes first of all the communion of love between the three Persons of the divine Trinity. That communion is the prototype or the supreme model for the communion between human persons in the body of Christ through the power of the Holy Spirit. In an ecclesiological perspective koinonia includes the eucharistic communion between all reconciled with God and among themselves. In this sense the fellowship of the churches gathered in the WCC or in any other ecumenical organization cannot be described as koinonia. In other words the concept of koinonia cannot be completely translated either with fellowship or with *Gemeinschaft* in German, or with other similar terms in modern languages.

From our point of view the fellowship of all member churches in the WCC cannot be described as koinonia, as long as those churches cannot partake of the same eucharist. We cannot accept speaking about degrees of koinonia in this context, or of an incomplete koinonia, because in that case we will accept a reduction of the importance of eucharistic communion for the unity of the church. On the other hand the fact that the churches in membership with the WCC believe in Jesus Christ as Lord and Saviour and confess the love of the Father and the fellowship of the Holy Spirit should be recognized as a fellowship which still needs to be qualified, as indicated in one of the recommendations of the Special Commission, but this fellowship cannot be described or understood as koinonia and even less as an incomplete koinonia.

As for the unity of the church we should mention that the Orthodox theologians recommended from the beginning as model and goal for that unity or as the way for re-establishing the visible unity of the churches, the unity of the church in the first Christian millennium. That does not mean going back, in time, but an effort to achieve the presence of Christ as a whole *(totus Christus)* in the inner lives of all believers of all churches. For Dumitru Staniloae, the re-establishing *(Wiederherstellung)* of the visible unity of the church is not merely an external matter, but an internal one, which seeks the existential confessing of faith in the integral Christ and of his revelation and not only a part of it. [16]

The unity of the church is to be redefined in relation to its diversity. In other terms the question still to be considered is concerning the limits of diversity, or even which will be the criteria for a legitimate diversity. The early church had to face different local traditions and in the end the most difficult task was to establish criteria in order to identify the true apostolic local traditions which belong to the unity of the one church of Jesus Christ and to reject those traditions which did not have apostolic roots. The unity of the church we all long for cannot include diversities, which exclude each other. In this respect we need criteria for the legitimate diversity within the unity which the churches of today want to re-establish. In this sense we can speak about "transformation of the churches" and only in this respect can we pray to God and ask him to transform the churches towards the unity He gave to his church from the beginning.

Some final remarks

In Orthodox perspective, ecclesiology should remain a central theme for the WCC and for the Faith and Order commission, respectively. In order to promote dialogue on that theme, texts like the paper on "The Nature and Purpose of the Church" are not enough. This paper is indeed only "a stage on the way to a common statement" and in this sense a very useful working tool. We would ask the Faith and Order commission to overcome the stage of simply exposing the different ecclesiological views one next to another as "for some", "others" and "thus some". The different views should be brought into dialogue in order to see how far they are legitimate diversities to be brought into a consensus.

The final report and the follow-up of the Special Commission should be taken into further consideration by the Orthodox churches. Along this path there are new possibilities for theological dialogue between the Orthodox churches and the other churches within the WCC inclusively on the theme of ecclesiology. In that respect the bilateral theological dialogues between the Orthodox churches and the other church families should also be taken more coherently into consideration.

The churches of the Reformation achieved considerable pulpit and eucharistic fellowship in the last decades, as is the case with the Leuenberg Church Fellowship (1973), today the Community of Evangelical Churches in Europe; the Porvoo Common Agreement (1993) between the British and Irish Anglican churches and the Nordic and Baltic Lutheran churches, the Meissen Agreement (1988) between the Church of England and the Evangelical Church in Germany; and Reuilly Common Agreement (2001) between the Protestant churches in France and the Church of England, the Anglican Church in Ireland and the Episcopal Church in Scotland. The Orthodox churches should take these agreements into consideration and start a theological dialogue with them in order to progress together on the way towards the visible unity of all churches of Christ in the whole world.

NOTES

[1] Metropolitan Gennadios of Sassima, "'God, in Your Grace, Transform the World': An Orthodox Approach", in *The Ecumenical Review*, vol. 56, no. 5, July 2004, p.288.

[2] *The Nature and Purpose of the Church: A Stage on the Way to a Common Statement*, Faith and Order Paper no. 181, WCC, 1998, p.31.

[3] *Church, Kingdom, World: The Church as Mystery and Prophetic Sign*, Gennadios Limouris ed., Faith and Order Paper no. 130, WCC, 1986, p.55.

[4] Dumitru Staniloae, *The Experience of God*, Ioan Ioniță and Robert Barringer trans. and eds, Brookline MA, Holy Cross Orthodox Press, pp.57-8.

[5] See Grigorios Larentzakis, "The One Church and Its Unity: Some Considerations from the Viewpoint of Orthodox Theology", paper delivered at the CEC-Leuenberg consultation on ecclesiology, Wittenberg, Germany, June 2004, p.10.

[6] André Scrima, *The Holy Spirit and the Unity of the Church: Diary of the Council* (in Romanian), Bucharest, Editura Anastasia, 2004, p.43.

[7] Groupe des Dombes, *For the Conversion of the Churches*, James Greig trans., WCC Publications, 1993, p.1.

[8] *Ibid.*, p.4.

[9] *Ibid.*, p.28.

[10] *The Nature and Purpose of the Church*, p.20.

[11] *Ibid.*, p.26.

[12] "Encyclical of the Ecumenical Patriarchate of Constantinople to the Churches of Christ in Every Place", 1920, in *The Ecumenical Movement: An Anthology of Key Texts and Voices*, Michael Kinnamon and Brian E. Cope eds, Geneva and Grand Rapids MI, WCC Publications and Eerdmanns, 1997, pp.11-14.

[13] *The Nature and Purpose of the Church*, p.28.

[14] See www.orthodoxresearchinstitute.org

[15] See www.cec-kek.org/English/ArmeniaE

[16] See Dumitru Staniloae, *Orthodoxe Dogmatik*, II. Band, Hermann Pitters trans., Benziger, 1990, p.207.

The Orthodox Tradition and Transfigurative Ethics

Reflections on the Ninth Assembly Theme

REV. DR KONDOTHRA M. GEORGE

And on the mountain, he was bright as the lightning and became more luminous than the sun initiating us into the mystery of the future. [1]

St Gregory the Theologian

Transfiguration of Jesus as narrated in the gospels (Matt. 17:1-8; Mark 9:2-13; Luke 9:28-36) occupies a central place in the theology and spirituality of the Eastern church. In addition to its literal, physical and spiritual meaning in the incarnate life of our Saviour, *transfiguration* has become a key metaphor for the theological–ethical reflection of the Orthodox churches. As a foretaste of the resurrected glory of Christ it hints at the eschatological vocation of all created reality. Orthodox theology has the task of exploring spiritually and theologically the connection between the ultimate experience of the "kingdom reality" and our daily experience of the "world reality". Transfiguration as event and metaphor provides the heuristic key.

In some predominant classical philosophical perceptions of pre-Christian or non–Christian origin, like for example the Greek Platonic or Indian *advaita* system, the world we encounter daily has a certain degree of illusory or not-so-real character. Its dubious reality arises from the fact that the knowledge of the world we receive through our senses is not dependable. It is subject to error, change, contradiction and confusion. It is in fact non-knowledge or ignorance *(a-vidya)*, and it results in the deceptive perception of the world known under innumerable names and forms. This not-so-real "aesthetic" or sense-based world is contrasted with the "noetic" (from *nous* – mind, intellect) world, which is stable and permanent and therefore real and dependable. When we arrive at the real knowledge the non-real fades away.

One possible consequence of this distinction, at least in the dominant Hindu religious philosophy, appears to be that the world of everyday reality with its pain and suffering, with its many forms of injustice and oppression, and with its ethical questions and moral puzzles, may be underestimated or totally ignored as of no real value.

Learned fathers of the church like the Cappadocians accepted the ancient philosophical distinction between the sensible world and the intellectual world, though they were careful not to underestimate or ignore the reality of our world, and to fall into a dichotomy inordinately glorifying the intellectual/spiritual world at the expense of the sensible/material world. They were helped in this by their firm faith in the mystery of the incarnation of God in Christ. That God, out of love for us *(philanthropia)*, assumed our human nature with its material matrix in order to save it, is the basis and guarantee of our Christian attitude to the world of the senses and of daily experience. If the Son of God, our Saviour, supremely manifested God's loving care, compassion and tender mercy to the created world in his incarnate life on earth, we are bound by love to exercise in all freedom our love, compassion and care for the world. This, in all simplicity, is the basis and driving force of the church's involvement in society and its commitment to a just world order. This is the incarnate and world-affirming character of the Christian faith.

Having said this, we should also admit that the Christian faith does not recognize the "form" or figure of the present world as ultimate. "Do *not* be conformed *(suschematizesthe)* to this world", exhorts the apostle Paul, "but be transformed *(metamorphousthe)* by the renewing of your minds, so that you may discern what is the will of God – what is good and acceptable and perfect" (Rom. 12:2). It is the scheme, design, pattern, form or mind-set of the present age that is to be shunned by Christians. We should not fit into it precisely because it is a false form that distorts the will of God and all that is good and beautiful. Hence the quest for *transformation*, going beyond or changing the form of this world.

Our search for the "new heaven and new earth" means that we are constantly seeking ever-new levels of reality. This process of transformation happens internally within our minds and externally in the order of society and in the very nature of material creation.

Conforming to the image

Reflecting on the task of Orthodox theology in the new millennium, Bishop Kallistos (Ware) wrote, "What is required more than anything else is a fuller understanding of the human person."[2]

At the core of the process of transfiguration is the human person who is created in God's image. Being "priest of creation" and the "mediator" between the spiritual and the material, the human being is called to conform to the image (icon) of the Son of God (Rom. 8:29). The increasing tendency to isolate the human person from the rest of creation has been a major trait of the domineering (Western) civilization ever since the Renaissance. By the time of the Enlightenment, fragmentation acquired legitimacy even within the human person by asserting the rational element as supreme at the expense of other human faculties. This was continued in different ways in the contemporary discussion in ecumenical and theological circles about human sexuality, sexual orientation, gender and rights. Because of the Orthodox conviction that "as human beings we are saved not from but *with* the world", Orthodox theology felt ill at ease with some of the highly individualistic and fragmentary assumptions of theological anthropology developed in the late 20th century.

The Orthodox world-view is decisively shaped by the event of incarnation. God's assuming our human nature and transforming it to be a partaker in God's own ineffable nature is the unique vantage point for Orthodoxy to "perceive" reality. It is the unique starting point for all our social action and involvement. Orthodox Christian anthropology is Christologically rooted and is therefore about an *Immanuel-ology*, or a *God-with-us-humanity*, and not simply a *human-ology*. Therefore, we cannot begin our reflection on human nature and destiny simply from a so-called "secular" human point of view or a "natural" human angle.

In the various streams of ecological thinking efforts are being made to correct the western *dominus* (lord) model of the human that has been dictating the shape of modern western/global civilization and its anthropocentric world-view until today. Sometimes this well-meaning effort seems to be carried to an extreme of undermining the specific role and call of the human being in creation. In "deep ecology", as opposed to anthropocentric "shallow ecology", human beings are just like any other organism in creation, having no special status or mission. The implications of this view can be dangerous in the long run in spite of its compassionate identification with the rest of creation. The patristic teaching about the priestly or mediatorial role of human beings in creation as the Image of God and as sons/daughters participating in God's grace and glory is ignored here. It is, therefore, the urgent task of the Orthodox churches to reaffirm their incarnational anthropology, eschewing the unchristian extremes of anthropocentrism and "anthropofugalism", and interpret anew God's image in humanity in response to the ecological as well as gender challenges facing us. As Metropolitan John (Zizioulas) of Pergamon reminds us, "It is in the human being that we must seek the link between God and the world and it is precisely this that makes man responsible, the only being, in a sense, responsible for the fate of creation."[3]

Originating in God's creative will and love, redeemed and transformed by God's compassionate act in Christ, working together with the Holy Spirit to transfigure God's creation, serving and co-existing with God's world in all humility, humanity has its genuine role as God's image and likeness. In an inclusive way, humanity should compassionately share its divine image with the rest of creation, just as God philanthropically shares the divine nature with us through Christ our Lord. Instead of the contemporary extremes of both nature-devastation and nature-worship, humanity can freely enter into a deep fellowship with God's creation taking it along in a common pilgrimage of transfiguration. St Gregory Nazianzen would point to a model for this when he speaks of the soul taking along the body as a fellow-servant *(homodoulos)* in the process of deification.

Our search for justice, peace and the well-being of creation is ultimately a search for the biblical vision of a new heaven and a new earth where "justice is at home" (2 Pet. 3:13; Rev. 21:1). The spiritual character and quality of our present struggle for a new world order "where justice dwells" is undergirded by its eschatological character. The ecumenical movement in the 20th century has been particularly sensitive (though not always with the eschatological underpinning) to a large spectrum of questions of justice and peace, from apartheid and racism to globalization and from rights of indigenous people to intellectual property rights. The bold witness of the churches in situations of oppression and viola-tion of human rights has been understood as constituting a "spirituality for our times". Here again it is our understanding of the human nature and its call and destiny that is the key to the many forms of Christian witness. As H.H. Aram I reminds us, "We cannot divorce the witness to Christ from the struggle for jus-tice and peace, and all human values and rights which constitute the *dignitas hominis* in human being. Human rights are integral to Christian faith."[4]

Violence and peace-making

"Transformative justice", as the struggle is called in a WCC resource guide,[5] has implications for the world context, since the ecumenical movement has always highlighted the vision of a global community. Whether we like it or not, globalization is affecting all our local communities in different forms of exclusion, marginalization and destruction of the environment. The cultural impact is even more dangerous and long-lasting since it attacks the fundamen-tal values of the integrity of family, personal morality, social ethics and the sacredness of God's gifts to humanity. While time-tested values and ways of life are actively disrupted, new "values" of competition and consumerism, profit and pleasure are promoted as the new ethics of success and happiness. Although our common sense knowledge tells us that our world is not simply sustainable if we adopt this kind of short-sighted and profligate life-style, the formidable engines of our new global civilization operate with such power that hardly anyone can resist. One of the most tangible consequences of the economic-cultural global-ization is the drastic increase in violence. The unprecedented disparity between the rich and the poor, both at national and international levels, the aggressive competition and the lustful array of luxury consumer goods generate interper-sonal and collective violence in formerly peaceful social settings, especially in developing countries. Very often the economic elements involved in the syndrome of violence are closely associated with religious, national, racial and cultural identities, and the situation goes beyond the control of political and reli-gious authorities.

The usual political answer to organised violence and terrorism is counter-vio-lence of war and weapons of mass destruction. As sociologist Peter Berger says, "violence is the ultimate foundation of any political order". Military expenditure of most of our countries, both rich and poor, far exceeds the amount spent on welfare. Last year 956 billion dollars were spent by the nations for military pur-poses. It is estimated that an annual ten percent of the world's military spending is enough to eradicate poverty and child mortality due to malnutrition and to pro-vide universal primary education to the world population by 2015. But the pri-orities of the powerful take a totally unjustifiable and unethical turn. As we wit-ness every day in places like Iraq, a violent political answer to violence does not solve the conflict but engenders an unending series of "terrorist" acts. Nobel Peace Prize laureate and Costa Rican political leader Oscar Arias said in a recent meeting of the Alliance for New Humanity, "Every conflict that is resolved through dialogue is a step forward. Every conflict that is resolved through violence leaves behind a trail of hatred and wounds that is very difficult to heal." [6]

The chain of evil and of good

The present networking of humanity through information technology into a global community has, along with its positive aspects, generated an insidious network of evil. In innumerable, very subtle and unprecedented ways evil forces are being globalized. Though some political leaders would name and identify the "axis of evil" with a few countries they do not like ideologically, the axis is cutting through the daily lives of all people on earth and is ironically perpetrated by the powerful and self-righteous nations. Some well-meaning Christians would correct and reinterpret the political-ideological content of "axis of evil" as "endemic poverty, devastation of the environment and the weapons of mass destruction". In a recent book Wesley Ariarajah would argue for an alternate "axis of peace" with the three major components of justice as the condition of peace, reconciliation as the way to peace and non-violence as the hope for peace. [7]

The globalized chain of evil concomitant with the economic-cultural globalization process reminds one of the *akolouthia* (chain or sequence) of evil described by St Gregory of Nyssa in the 4th century. "Men always attaching evil to evil extend evil into a flowing stream." [8] This is like a chain reaction. The only alternative is to break the chain of evil by the chain of good. This is what Christ has initiated for us, opening the way of salvation. We are not to confront violence by violence, but as the Lord taught us, respond to evil by good, and to curse by blessing. "Evil happenings can be counteracted only by their opposite. And evil words and actions would not have developed to such a pitch if some kind word or deed had intervened to break the continuity of the chain of evil." [9]

Seeking the alternatives

Reflecting and acting on the *alternative* is more important than brooding over the cancer of evil. St Gregory the Theologian assures us that "evil has no substance or kingdom". Evil is the absence of the good, and therefore has no substantial existence though it frightens and puts us into confusion by its manifestation in our experience. Our search for alternatives is based on this ultimate faith in overcoming evil. The early church's self-understanding was that it was an *altera civitas*, another city, not conformed to this world, but prefiguring the heavenly Jerusalem. The ascetic-monastic movement in the 3rd century revived this idea when the official church was suspected to be conforming itself to the world. In the course of history, that movement also became more or less rigidly institutionalized though its vitality was not completely lost. Today, because of their rich theological and spiritual resources, the Orthodox churches have a special responsibility to provide guidance to the ecumenical movement in its commitment to the transformation of the world. Our churches can certainly join hands with others in a renewed search for viable and just alternatives to heal the

wounds of the present age and make a breakthrough for humanity in its contemporary spiritual impasse.

In the ancient monastic alternative, the "law-givers" of that tradition like St
Basil of Caesarea favoured and encouraged the communal style of life over the
solitary way, in spite of the great reputation of solitary ascetics like St Antony in
the 3rd century. The main reason for their clear preference for the communal
ideal was that Christian virtues of an individual spiritual seeker could be tested
and perfected only in a community. The solitary ascetic, however genuine in
intention, has no means of proving his mettle, and consequently could indulge
in self-righteous subjectivism, thus destroying his spiritual life. The community
ideal thus indicated that on the one hand, one's soul has to be trained and
trimmed for the kingdom, and on the other hand, one should be necessarily open
to the give and take with the Other. This monastic ideal is paradigmatic for the
historical life of the church and its social involvement. The church's mission and
witness are not an exercise in solipsism, but opening up to God's world with a
view to its transfiguration. It is in this process that the church's vocation to be
the body and the bride of Christ is being fully realized.

Ultimately the alternative is the vision of a new civilization rooted in a new
self-understanding of the human. Metropolitan Paulos Mar Gregorios spells out
some of the parameters of a new enlightenment and an alternate vision:

> In this alternative perception of reality, the centrality of the humanity will not, as in
> the secular perception, be of a domineering nature, but will be entirely mediatorial,
> i.e. manifesting wisdom, power, glory, beauty, goodness and love, not humanity's
> own, but wholly dependent upon and derived from the Transcendent, as well as
> embodying in ourselves the whole universe as we offer it up along with our own
> living selves to the Transcendent in loving adoration. [10]

Conclusion

In conclusion, the following elements for a *transfigurative* ethics may be
given special attention by our churches on the basis of the biblical-patristic heritage of the Orthodox Tradition:

1. *Humanity:* It is our task to rediscover and articulate what is truly human
   amidst pressures of the secular and liberal Christian streams to manipulate
   our God-given humanity through various "orientations" and deterministic
   perceptions that distort or deny true human freedom.

2. *Healing:* The Orthodox approach to the violence of the present age is to be
   therapeutic, following the incarnational model involving God's compassion,
   care, corrective discipline, reconciliation and forgiveness. Salvation of the
   world is the ultimate direction of all social action.

3. *Hospitality:* There is no way the Orthodox Tradition can escape or sideline
   God's creation. We are bound to receive the stranger, the passer-by and the
   excluded. This has profound theological implications for justice, peace and

the well-being of creation. God's *philanthropia* to us humans and our *philoxenia* to our fellow humans are two sides of the same coin.

4. *Localness:* The local church concept is not to be reduced to a mere juridical-ecclesiastical practice, but creatively correlated to the contextual missionary tasks and socio-cultural initiatives necessitated by the actual life of our faithful in diverse situations. A spirituality of the locus as particular and holistic *(katholike)* could be an antidote to the false globalism of the present age.

5. *Communion:* Ultimately the communion of love compels us to think over our ecclesiastical structures that impede sacramental communion even when we share common faith in the triune mystery and the incarnate Christ, and encourages us to explore with others ways of seriously moving to visible unity, however modest and provisional.

Christ's transfiguration "initiated us into the mystery of the future" as Gregory the Theologian reminds us. We need to travel joyfully together on the way to that future which is nothing but the fulfilment of the kingdom of God.

NOTES

[1] Gregory of Nazianzus, *Oration* XXX.19.

[2] Kallistos of Diokleia, "The Witness of the Orthodox Church in the Twentieth Century", *Sourozh*, 80, May 2000.

[3] Metropolitan John of Pergamon, "Preserving God's Creation", Part II, *Sourozh*, 82, 2000, pp.31-40.

[4] Aram I, *The Christian Witness at the Crossroads in the Middle East*, Armenian Catholicosate of Cilicia, Antelias, Lebanon, 2004, p.32.

[5] *Transformative Justice: Being Church and Overcoming Racism*, resource guide, JPC team, WCC, 2004.

[6] Oscar Arias, "Dialogue and Disarmament for Liberty", speech delivered at second meeting of Alliance for a New Humanity, San Juan, Puerto Rico, Dec. 2004.

[7] S. Wesley Ariarajah, *The Axis of Peace: Christian Faith in Times of Violence and War*, WCC Publications, 2004, pp.111f.

[8] Gregory of Nyssa, *In Inscriptions Psalmorum*. See for an interpretation of the akolouthia of evil and of good in Nyssa, Paulos Gregorios, *Cosmic Man: The Divine Presence*, New Delhi, Sophia, 1980, pp.61f.

[9] Gregory of Nysaa, *Contra Eunomium*, Book I, PG 45, 277B.

[10] Paulos Mar Gregorios, "Towards a New Enlightenment", address given at Chicago 100th anniversary of Parliament of Religions, Aug. 1993.

"God, in Your Grace, Transform the Whole Creation"

Ecology and Environmental Issues and Challenges

MS KATERINA KARKALA-ZORBA

It is with joy and also great emotion that I am addressing you today. It is always a joy to welcome so many Orthodox friends and representatives from other member churches of the World Council of Churches in Greece, my homeland, and also to meet some good friends again. But it is also with great emotion, since I am standing here in front of you, in order to invite you to reflect on an important subject, namely certain aspects of God's presence in the world, which is also the theme of the next assembly of the World Council of Churches, planned for February 2006 in Porto Alegre.

We are very happy to be gathered here in order to prepare, as Orthodox, the way to this big event and we all are very grateful to His Eminence, the Metropolitan of Rhodes Kyrillos, for his kindness in inviting us to his diocese which is under the jurisdiction of the Ecumenical Patriarchate. We are very grateful to His All Holiness the Ecumenical Patriarch of Constantinople Bartholomew for this possibility given to us all to meet and exchange our views on the way to the next WCC assembly. The theme of the next assembly, "God, in Your Grace, Transform the World", is very close to the concerns of His All Holiness, since he is very well known for his care for the environment – if I might remind you of the consultation on the ship in the Mediterranean, Baltic and other seas and many other important steps towards the preservation of creation.

Rhodes is a milestone in the ecumenical movement, where also other important conferences have taken place in the past. I have in mind the pan-Orthodox consultation on the place of women in the Orthodox church in 1988.[1] And as in those days, also now His Eminence Gennadios of Sassima is here as a guarantee that the follow-up will happen. Together with George Lemopoulos, deputy general secretary of WCC, Teny Pirri-Simonian, programme executive of Church and Ecumenical Relations, and other WCC staff members this meeting was prepared, and I am grateful for having been invited to address you.

Introduction to the theme

I am sure that I will not be able to offer much that is new, since you will certainly have your own remarks and reflections. Rather, I would like to examine together with you how God is transforming or transfiguring creation. I also would like to recall that we find ourselves in a period of our common church life according to the church calendar, where we would situate perhaps the most this transformation or transfiguration of God of the whole creation: the incarnation of the Logos and Word of God, known as Christmas, the birth of the Son of God, who was made human. It is out of the light of the new-born Christ, just one week ago for those on the old calendar and three weeks ago for those on the new calendar. It is out of this "epiphanic aspect" of our church life that I will speak to you today. Epiphany is the revelation of God as triune, since the Greek word *epifainomai* means revelation. But it is also fulfilled in the resurrection and shown beforehand at the transfiguration or metamorphosis (in Greek), which means a reshaping of human nature. One could think that God shows his glory in Epiphany, where the human being is taken over through baptism in order to get transfigured and longs for the resurrection. This is the path of God's intervention in creation and it is also through his grace that He transforms creation, not only human beings, but also animals, plants, the whole cosmos.

Finally, we are gathered here at a very difficult time for the world, after the disaster of the tsunami in Asia. The whole world watched with fear the anger of the waves on the coasts of the Asian islands and still the waves have not calmed down. Let us hope that we will not have any further natural catastrophe of this measure so soon again.

Orthodox theology of creation

In the Orthodox understanding the world was created ex nihilo. God is not a "décorateur" of creation, but has created the world, out of his will. The church fathers, like St Maximus the Confessor[2] and St Basil the Great, have written about the fact that God is not the one who has invented just the shapes and forms, but the nature of all creatures.[3] The trinitarian aspect in creation is very important, since it is the will of God the Father, who through the Word/Logos of God, in the breathing of the Holy Spirit, creates everything. St Gregorius Palamas goes further when he speaks of the energy of God, which makes the creation ex nihilo not only a new created reality, but also the result of the energy of God; it is a dynamic aspect, which fulfils the aim in the perspective of the Creator. Paul writes in his letter to the Romans that "God calls into existence things that did not exist before" (Rom. 4:17).

Out of this understanding of creation, it is obvious that creation does not exist alone and is not independent or autonomous of God the Creator. Creation is rather in a direct link to the Creator and the raison d'être of creation is finally in the Creator himself.[4] God has created the visible (material) and invisible (spiritual) world, as we confess in our creed. The human being is participating in the visible as well as in the invisible world and is somehow the link between both, since the human being is both material and spiritual. The world was created in order to glorify in the acts of God his endless wisdom and strength and perfection.

Because of this, the world has no value in itself, but only in relationship to its Creator. The meaning of the creation is not to be found in itself, but, as an act of its Creator, the creation is referring to God and to the human being made in the image and likeness of God. Therefore, the created nature cannot exist without the relation to the human being and God.

Creation and fall

The creation in the image of the Creator is "good" ("and God saw that it was good", Gen. 1:25). But after the fall of the first created human beings, Adam and Eve, the "whole nature has been groaning in travail together until now" (Rom. 8:22). Therefore, it is the whole creation which is longing and looking for its salvation. The human being and the created world cannot be seen separated, and therefore the human being is the one who is responsible to take care of it, to cultivate it and to be its steward.

In fact the whole creation is suffering under the present situation. Humanity is certainly responsible for the changes in our climate, disparities of species, decreasing resources, water supplies, etc. And certainly humanity, like the natural environment, suffers from disasters and natural catastrophes, like the recent tsunami, but also from disasters and destruction caused by war and armed conflicts.

Where is God in this whole situation? How does He interfere or act in order to help us to detect his will in all this? How can He let it all happen? Those questions are asked very frequently, especially by young people or children, but also by adults who are questioning themselves or people in church structures.

Divine economy and creation

But God so loved the world that He sent his only Son to us to save not only human beings, but also the whole of creation. In the first message of the Ecumenical Patriarch Bartholomew I, for the feast of nativity in 1991, he refers to the meaning of the nativity of our Lord Jesus Christ, "who became flesh for all (humankind and nature)".

In the wonderful texts of nativity and epiphany, we see this very clearly:

> Thy nativity, O Christ our God, hath shined the light of knowledge upon the world; for thereby they that worshipped the stars were instructed by a star to worship Thee, the Sun of Righteousness, and to know Thee, the Dayspring from on high. O Lord, glory be to Thee.[5]

The prayers of epiphany show the character of the feast, namely to show the act of sanctification of the Holy Spirit:

> O merciful King, do Thou now be present through the descent of thy Holy Spirit, and sanctify this water... and give to it the grace of redemption, the blessing of Jordan. Make it a source of in-corruption, a gift of sanctification, a ransom from sins, a guard against sickness, a defence against devils, inaccessible to every adverse power, and filled with angelic strength. "Do thou therefore, O Master, sanctify now this water, by thy Holy Spirit... give sanctification, blessing, cleansing, and health to all those touched, anointed, and partaking thereof.

In Jesus Christ human beings become the new creation, they become what "they are supposed to be – the image and likeness of God – and to live in fellowship and communion with God".[6] It is through and in Jesus, through his incarnation and in his resurrection that human beings, but also the whole creation, get this new possibility of re-creation. Christ's resurrection is a hope for every human being to overcome death in the struggle against evil and a guarantee "for the salvation of every person and the entire creation".[7]

In the Holy Spirit, given to us in the sacraments of the church, as well as in every sanctifying action of the church, and with the grace of God, Christians receive their hope and "see their responsibility to transfigure creation in both spiritual and material ways".[8]

Transfiguration in God's grace

St Symeon the New Theologian stressed the point on the eucharistic cosmology or the eucharistic use of the world.[9] The created world is not separated from humankind. We would rather confirm that neither could the one or the other achieve salvation alone, but only in relationship to one another. God's sanctifying actions embrace creation in its whole, humankind and natural environment. This is being made visible in epiphany and in every sanctifying act, since nature is taking part in the sanctifying of the waters, in the use of material like oil, grapes, water, wood or other material for ecclesiastical use, etc. Even in the highest of all moments, in the holy eucharist, the priest and the ecclesiastical community has nothing more to bring to God, but what belongs to him: "Thine own of thine own we offer unto Thee". We cannot offer anything higher and more precious to God, than bread and wine, flesh and blood of his own Son. Finally, it is true that "we do not own creation but are the free agents through whom creation is offered to the Creator".[10]

As we experience every time anew in epiphany and in every blessing of the waters, nature does not only become the vehicle of this blessing (namely the element water), but is rather more incorporated in the doxological part of it. Jordan, the river, gets a human face. We ask in our hymns questions such as, "Jordan river, why are you astonished in front of the vision of God coming into you?", or "the waters have seen you and have been frightened".[11] The triune God shows himself in all his glory, He reveals his divinity during the baptism of Jesus. He uses the natural elements in order to do this and brings about the "transformation" of the whole world, as we can see in the hymns of epiphany:

> Lord, when You were baptized in the Jordan, the veneration of the Trinity was revealed. For the voice of the Father gave witness to You, calling You Beloved, and the Spirit, in the guise of a dove, confirmed the certainty of his words. Glory to You, Christ our God, who appeared and enlightened the world.

It is through the descent of the Holy Spirit that the world is being sanctified. God transforms the creation by sanctifying it. It is this spiritual dimension of creation which is given back to it by the Creator himself, by offering his Son to humankind.

There is no salvation for the human being without the salvation of the whole cosmos. In the sacrament of baptism it is through the water that the human being is sanctified and becomes a part of the body of Jesus Christ. "As many of you have been baptized into Christ have put on Christ" (Gal. 3:27). Anointed with the holy myron the new member of the church is now bound with this new testimony and through the participation at the sacraments, the cycle of prayer and the ascetic life, the human body is in the cycle of transformation or transfiguration from the corrupt body to the transfigured and to be resurrected with Jesus Christ.

At the moment of his transfiguration, Jesus showed his glory to his disciples. He showed them the human body transfigured, as it will be after his resurrection. It is human nature which is here, transformed or transfigured, [12] and by this the whole creation can take part in this process. It is not only a spiritual sanctification, but also a transformation of the material body. After the writings of St Gregory Palamas [13] that the divine nature of Jesus did not abandon him even after his crucifixion and burial of three days, the divine grace does not abandon the human being during his life and even his death.

Ecological crisis and God's presence

The attempts of humanity today to destroy the environment, to poison it, to violate nature, are acts guided by the one who is separating the world from the will and the grace of God, by the evil one, the διάβολος. [14] It is the one who in paradise and still today wants to persuade human beings that they alone are the governors of this world. For the church fathers, everything that is destroying or defaming creation is equal with the triumph of the evil in this world and announces the coming of Antichrist and the end of this world, as described in the book of Revelation. [15]

As we have seen earlier, the creation of the world "out of nothing" is not a result in itself, which can act independently and autonomously from the Creator. God and the world are interlinked. Creation comes into being with the intervention of God the Creator. Therefore, any attempt to change creation without or outside of the will of God, is ephemeral and destructive. One could even go further and say that the destruction of the environment is a serious sin and an offence towards God, as His All Holiness the Ecumenical Patriarch Bartholomew I stated in his message on the 1 September 1994 for the day of the protection of the creation. [16] The destruction and the pollution of the environment are insulting the holiness of the world and God himself, who has been revealed in creation and is adored through the offering of Creation. [17]

It is not out of hatred towards the environment that the human being is acting in this destructive way, but because of his or her inner weakness, caused by the threat of death. These fears make human existence lose its faith in the divine intervention in this world, which causes feelings of insecurity and uncertainty. [18] Without faith in God, nourished by the security of the relationship between Creator and creation, the creative activity of the human being is dominated by selfishness and anxiety. It is out of these feelings that we have to understand the misuse and the illogical use of natural resources, the destruction of nature, the pollution of the waters, etc., but also the selfishness of some people wanting more privileges than others, accumulating goods in the hands of some people, having people starving to death in some countries, while in others people are overweight and spend enormous sums of money in diet centres.

How can we today overcome this crisis and become again the keepers and stewards of creation for its sake and also for our sake? How can the environment, the world and we human beings in general get transformed in the grace of God and become "good" again, as God has created us?

Nature and transcendence

We surely know that nothing in this world is everlasting: neither riches nor beauty, neither privileges nor glory. Everything is relative and everything perishes. Even time and space have the same destiny. As we have experienced during the recent tremendous catastrophes in Asia, nature can destroy in a few seconds what human beings have built up for years. We are helpless in front of natural disasters, even today in the age of high technology and perfection in electronic and medical analysis. Any outbreak of this vicious cycle would therefore also mean to transcend the relativity of this world, to go against the rules of this world.

All the sacraments and the prayers of our church want to transcend this cycle and even to go "against" nature. The sacrament of baptism shows this literally when the godfather or the godmother is spitting on the evil one in order to take over the new nature. It is bringing back the corrupt nature to the first created by God, before the fall.

It is also the same effort being fulfilled by the ascetic tradition and the monastic life. It is an effort to "kill" the ego, the needs for earthly goods in order to restore the authentic needs of the body and the soul. Through prayer, communication to God and to other people and also to the whole creation is restored, too. In the biographies of the ascetics in the desert of Egypt, Mount Athos and the frozen Steppe, beyond the Volga, we can read that wild animals enter into dialogue in their own way with the ascetics, men and women, without harming them at all.

The role of the church

One of the main theses of the Orthodox theology of creation is the reconciliation of the human being with the environment, nature. Reconciliation with the fallen nature makes hatred and wildness disappear. Here is also the work or mystery of the church: she is embracing everything, visible and invisible, in a transcendent unity. Human beings and creation are sanctified in the "churchification" process [19] of the whole cosmos. The spiritual is united again with the material, which is finally sanctified. Through the Holy Spirit, God is sanctifying the whole world, the creation, in his grace.

The only possible reconciliation of the human being with creation on earth is the mystery of the church, where the God-human and cosmic meeting is taking place: in the eucharistic koinonia. [20] It is as if the human being becomes finally a human being and nature finally nature. It is through the grace of God that creation can be transformed, transfigured, restored to what it was called to be: a place where God is glorified and praised. The wildness of nature is being quelled and the human being is not the dynast of this world, but rather the servant of the creator. It is only through the doxological and eucharistic anaphora (offering) of the human being and the world to God and finally the recapitulation and reconciliation with the primary creation in Christ, as we experience it in the ecclesiastic community, that we can fulfil the restoration of the whole world. [21]

Environment and ethical values

We could therefore state that by protecting the environment, we do not only want to preserve it, just because it is beautiful or because we need it, but because it belongs to God's creation, because it is a unique act of the Creator and a living organism and because humanity belongs to this creation, too. Human beings are in a constant relationship with the nature in a symbiotic and synergetic way. The way the earth is cultivated, the food prepared, the whole life-style of the human communities show the correct or incorrect use of natural goods.

The natural environment is not only the frame; the material goods have not only a unique value because of giving us resources and prime materials. We may look with wonder on glory of nature and admire natural phenomena, but nature has a value even in its lowest forms, earth, clay, sand and rocks. Everything has its own value, its own strength and longing for life. The natural environment is a special place, where human beings renewed in Jesus Christ can breathe anew.

But how is this possible in a world where on one side we speak of sustainable living and on the other we misuse the resources of our planet? [22] When on one side we live in a high consumer society and on the other side people die because of hunger, while only 30-49 percent have access to drinking water and 25-50 new-born children out of 1000 die immediately after being born, while less then 50 percent of the population have access to pharmaceutical and medical treatment. [23]

What would be the contribution of the church in view of the new or scientific development in biotechnology, food engineering and cloning? What is the position of the Orthodox church concerning biotechnology? And where is the difference to the "transformation" we ask God to perform in his grace in the world today?

Actual efforts of the Orthodox church to answer the ecological crisis

It is certainly of great interest to see what the position of the Orthodox church is and what efforts are made in order to answer the challenges of the ecological problems of today. [24]

First of all we have to state that the church is looking at all ecological problems as serious problems which affect the church and humanity and therefore they are part of the concerns of the church. We will refer here to some of those efforts, which show precisely this concern. Of course, we could add many others, according to one's own experience and testimony. And of course this is valuable not only for the Orthodox church, but also for other churches.

Since 1989 the ecclesiastical year is being set under the seal of the protection of the creation, by the late Ecumenical Patriarch Dimitrios I. Since then a special liturgy is celebrated on this day, with texts related to the protection of creation. All Orthodox and Christian churches are invited to participate in the prayers and intercessions of this day, as a thanksgiving for the great gift of the creation, but also as a supplication for its protection, sanctification and healing. All human beings are asked to respect the creation, to protect it and to pass this respect on to their children. All people in governing bodies are asked to take measures in order to protect the natural environment.

Many of the pan-Orthodox gatherings of recent years had on their agenda the theme of the environment, nature and creation. This was also true for the meeting of the hierarchs of all Orthodox churches in 1992 in Constantinople as well as other meetings, e.g. on the island of Patmos in 1989, in Crete in 1991, in Chalki in 1992 and also the seminars of the Orthodox Centre of the Ecumenical Patriarchate in Chambésy. Biological farming is a reality in Orthodox monasteries, like Ormylia in Chalkidiki, Chrysopigi in Chania/Crete, Saint John the Forerunner in Anatoli/Metropolie of Dimitrias and Almyros, etc. Many churches have special commissions and working groups on environmental and other issues. For example, the church of Greece has a special commission for the ecological problems of the holy synod and the institute for bio-ethics, where current and crucial issues on biotechnology are discussed and where theologians and scientists are confronted with the position of the church on such bio-ethical dilemmas and especially of the Genetically Modified Organisms. [25]

The Orthodox church is participating in all ecumenical meetings and assemblies of the WCC and CEC on the theme of justice, peace and integration of creation. We could cite the sixth assembly of the WCC in Vancouver in 1983, the first European Ecumenical Assembly in Basel in 1989, the seventh assembly of the WCC in Canberra in 1991, the second European Ecumenical Assembly in Graz in 1997, etc.

Orthodox participation is important in all those meetings and committees and is even asked for. The special contribution of the Orthodox church is the liturgical-eucharistic character of the intercessions and prayers in the divine liturgy, with their ecological character: we pray for the good winds, favourable weather, an abundance of the fruits of the earth, temperate seasons. The spiritual and ascetic character of the Orthodox church today is perhaps more important than ever before. This can be seen in the monasteries, but also during the periods of fasting and in periods like Great Lent before Easter, etc. It is like a changing lifestyle, which is proposed on different occasions to all people who want to follow it. For this repentance, metanoia is important. I have to repent of my sins, of my former life, in order to prepare to start a new life in and with Jesus Christ.

The Orthodox Tradition can offer to the world today another vision of looking at creation. How can we offer to our brothers and sisters "a word of hope and love, of consolation and solidarity, but more than this a word of truth", [26] in view of the conflicts and catastrophes in our world today? Fourteen years ago the

WCC prepared for the Canberra assembly under the theme "Come, Holy Spirit, Renew the Whole Creation". The Orthodox participants in the assembly stated at that time "that we have to be careful and watch in confusing the Holy Spirit with a 'private' spirit, the spirit of the world, or other spirits, since 'pneumatology' is not outside the teaching of the church on Christology, and the Holy Trinity, as it is confessed in the church and the divine revelation".[27]

The difference between activists and Christians regarding their common aim to preserve nature or creation respectively is that while the first have as their only aim the preservation of nature as such, the others have a reason for doing it, namely out of their responsibility for creation and their faith. The ecological and environmental issues do regard Christians as well, but the reason why differs from any other ecological organization. However, the challenges of today are different from those of yesterday. Christians are called today to answer not only with words, but also with actions on crucial ecological problems and questions. Are we prepared to do so? Can we go out of our "easy" life in order to adopt a sustainable development and life-style, as our church is asking us anyway?

Proposals

One could end here and leave it to the ecological ethic of every person to respond, or not to respond, to the challenges of today. But we could also look forward and make some concrete proposals in order not to wait for another tsunami and get ready for gathering charity support to people in distress or in difficult situations.

Such proposals might be:

1. To develop in our own parish or diocese an ecological conscience (initiating, for example, programmes for recycling). In fact for many of our societies such habits are not unknown, since it was the life-style of some generations ago. Today the consumer society has devastated all our countries and we are sometimes helpless in front of all the garbage we are gathering everyday. But a parish house, a church building, the yard of a church are certainly entities in which such an ecological conscience could be developed and become an example for all.

2. To cooperate with ecological organizations in our area. These organizations are ready to cooperate and can share their competence with people in the parishes. Common actions could be organized, as well as people from those organizations invited to speak in our parishes in order to pass on correct and topical information and raise awareness.

3. To learn how to act in an environmentally friendly way. No one is excused in neglecting the fact that the natural world is suffering. Everyone speaks of a "sustainable life-style", but how can this be put into practice? As Christians we do have an ascetic way of life, which is today rarely valid in our parishes, but more likely to be found in the monastic communities. We might also find nuns and monks who could help us to look for this other/sustainable life-style. This cannot be done without prayer and an ascetic life. To fast does not mean only to abstain from certain food, but also to develop a certain behaviour towards material goods.

4. To have a permanent door open in our parish for environmental catastrophes (earthquakes, floods, fire, etc.) and helping those people in distress. Clothing, food and medicament banks might help in such situations. Many churches have philanthropic organizations, like the International Orthodox Christian Charities (IOCC) in the USA with a worldwide network. Similar organizations exist also in the Patriarchates of Moscow, of Serbia, of Bulgaria, the Orthodox Church of Finland and others. The Church of Greece has "Solidarity", the philanthropic organisation,[28] which is helping many people, especially also the victims of the recent catastrophes in Asia. Other dioceses in Greece have houses for homeless people or a network of charities and doctors.[29]

5. And finally a very concrete proposal: According to the words of our Lord "for I was hungry and you gave me food, I was thirsty and you gave me drink, I was a stranger and you welcomed me, I was naked and you clothed me, I was sick and you visited me, I was in prison and you came to me" (Matt. 25:35-36), Christians should approach the fellow human being, whether he or she is in prison, in hospital or in distress. Today, we see the catastrophes in the poorest countries of our planet, where the very rich spend their holidays, exploiting and abusing poor people and children, where we count over 200,000 dead, 500,000 injured, 5 million people homeless – and these are only the first results. Once the first emotional shock has passed, one can imagine how long it will take until those people get back to normal life and ask, "Which normal life?" The one of poverty and dependence or the one a person in dignity before God and other human beings should have? After the catastrophe, the so-called developed countries have learned about the situation in those countries. We have seen and learned that the "system of natural catastrophes is linked to social classes".[30] All have responded in a very direct way in sending money, food and clothes to the afflicted countries. But more than this, those countries would need a way to "drop the debt" in order to rebuild a healthy society and help their environment to be rebuilt. How can we, as Christians, as churches act more concretely in this situation? This is the challenge for the church today to help in that direction and also to discover behind the material disasters also the need for helping people to find their faith in God in our world today.

Let us hope that such catastrophes will be an opportunity to pray once again to God and ask him again and again:

"God, in your Grace, transform the world". So it may be – Γένοιτο!

NOTES

[1] Cf. Gennadios Limouris ed., *The Place of the Woman in the Orthodox Church and the Question of the Ordination of Women*, inter-Orthodox consultation, Rhodes, Nov. 1988, Katerini, Tertios, 1992.

[2] Cf. Nikos Matsoukas, *Cosmos, Human Being, Society according to Maximos the Confessor*, Athens, 1980 (in Greek).

[3] Basil the Great, Homily to the Hexaimeron, Homely II, PG 29, 33.

[4] Cf. Nicolas Berdiaev, *Le Sens de la création*, Desclée De Brouwer, 1955.

5   Apolytikion of the Nativity.

6   Gennadios Limouris ed., *Justice, Peace and the Integrity of Creation: Insights from Orthodoxy*, WCC Publications, 1990, p.ix.

7   "Orthodox Perspectives of Creation", in Limouris, *Justice*, p.9.

8   Cf. op. cit.

9   Cf. Anestis Kesselopoulos, *Human Being and Natural Environment: Study on Saint Symeon the New Theologian*, Athens, Domos, 1992 (in Greek).

10   Orthodoxy and the Ecological Crisis, Ecumenical Patriarchate, assisted by the WWF, 1990.

11   Verses of Epiphany.

12   The Greek word is μεταμορφώνομαι, "to transfigure".

13   PG 150, 1093A, Decalogue of the law according to Christ.

14   From the Greek word διαβάλλω – "to separate, to defame".

15   Sarah Hobson and Sarah Lubchenco eds, Apocalypse and Environment, symposion in Patmos, 20-27 Sept. 1995.

16   Encyclical of His All Holiness on 1 Sept. 1994 for the Day of Protection of Creation.

17   Ilia Oikonomou, *Theological Ecology, Theory and Praxis*, D. Mavrommati ed., Athens, 1994. Cf. Photius the Great, Amfilochia.

18   Archbishop Christodoulos, "Life as Gift of God. Theology and Bioethics", speech in Iasi in Honour of Fr Dumitru Staniloae, 13 Oct. 2003 (in Greek).

19   In Greek: ἐκκλησιασμός.

20   John Zizioulas, *Eucharist, Bishop, Church: The Unity of the Church in the Divine Eucharist and the Bishop during the First Three Centuries*, trans. Elizabeth Theokritoff, Brookline MA, Holy Cross Orthodox Press, 2001. Cf. his *The Creation as Eucharist, Theological Approach of the Ecological Problem*, Athens, Akritas, 1992 (in Greek).

21   Cf. Konstantinos Zachos, *The Lost Intimacy: The Ecological Crisis in the Light of the Thought of Saint Maximos the Confessor*, Larissa, Ella/Terra Incognita (in Greek).

22   Cf. Ilia, *Theological Ecology*, p.289.

23   Figures of 9 Jan. 2005 in the Greek newspaper " Παρόν".

24   Cf. Konstantinos Zorbas, *Church and Natural Environment*, Katerini, Tertios, 1998 (in Greek).

25   Cf. Editions of the Institute for Bioethics of the Church of Greece: Archimandrite Nikolaos Chatzinikolaou [now Metropolitan of Mesogaias and Lavreotikis], *Liberated from the Gene*, Athens, 2002 (in Greek). Nikolaos Koios, *Ethical Review of the Technical Interventions on the Human Genes*, Athens, Centre of Bioethics, 2003 (in Greek).

26   Georges Lemopoulos ed., *The Seventh Assembly of the WCC, Canberra, February 1991*, Katerini, Tertios, 1992, p.15 (in Greek).

27   "Thoughts of the Orthodox Participants at the WCC Seventh Assembly in Canberra", in Lemopoulos, *The Seventh Assembly*, p.80.

28   For the social work of the Church of Greece, cf. Φιλανθρωπία. Ἔκδ. Ἀποστολική Διακονία τῆς Ἐκκλησίας τῆς Ἑλλάδος, Athens, 2000.

29   E.g. the diocese of Dimitrias and Almyros with a network of doctors of charity and plans for a station of first aid.

30   Jeffrey D. Sachs, director of the Earth Institute of the University of Columbia, "Time", in *Kathimerini*, 9 Jan. 2005, p.8 (in Greek).

Economic Injustice

BISHOP DR ATHANASIOS OF ACHAIA

For I am about to create new heavens and a new earth; the former things shall not be remembered or come to mind.

But be glad and rejoice forever in what I am creating; for I am about to create Jerusalem as a joy, and its people as a delight.

I will rejoice in Jerusalem, and delight in my people; no more shall the sound of weeping be heard in it, or the cry of distress.

No more shall there be in it an infant that lives but a few days, or an old person who does not live out a lifetime; for one who dies at a hundred years will be considered a youth, and one who falls short of a hundred will be considered accursed.

They shall build houses and inhabit them; they shall plant vineyards and eat their fruit.

They shall not build and another inhabit; they shall not plant and another eat; for like the days of a tree shall the days of my people be, and my chosen shall long enjoy the work of their hands.

They shall not labour in vain, or bear children for calamity; for they shall be offspring blessed by the Lord – and their descendants as well.

Before they call I will answer, while they are yet speaking I will hear.

The wolf and the lamb shall feed together, the lion shall eat straw like the ox; but the serpent – its food shall be dust! They shall not hurt or destroy on all my holy mountain, says the Lord.

Isaiah 65:17-25

"For the kingdom of heaven is like a landowner who went out early in the morning to hire labourers for his vineyard.

After agreeing with the laborers for the usual daily wage, he sent them into his vineyard.

When he went out about nine o'clock, he saw others standing idle in the marketplace;

and he said to them, "You also go into the vineyard, and I will pay you whatever is right." So they went.

When he went out again about noon and about three o'clock, he did the same.

And about five o'clock he went out and found others standing around; and he said to them, "Why are you standing here idle all day?"

They said to him, "Because no one has hired us." He said to them, "You also go into the vineyard."

When evening came, the owner of the vineyard said to his manager, "Call the labourers and give them their pay, beginning with the last and then going to the first."

When those hired about five o'clock came, each of them received the usual daily wage.

Now when the first came, they thought they would receive more; but each of them also received the usual daily wage.

And when they received it, they grumbled against the landowner,

saying, "These last worked only one hour, and you have made them equal to us who have borne the burden of the day and the scorching heat."

But he replied to one of them, "Friend, I am doing you no wrong; did you not agree with me for the usual daily wage? Take what belongs to you and go; I choose to give to this last the same as I give to you. Am I not allowed to do what I choose with what belongs to me? Or are you envious because I am generous? So the last will be first, and the first will be last."

Matthew 20:1-16

I am writing these lines under the influence of the news about the terrible disaster that has occurred in the Indian Ocean, just when Christians were in the mood to celebrate Christmas. In the aftermath, as the media were transmitting the news, we were much encouraged by moving acts of solidarity worldwide on behalf of men, women and children in utter poverty and desolation. We were also shocked by news about atrocities of despicable exploitation, and human aid that never reaches its destination. The grandeur of human feelings and inhuman meanness coexist in a world that injects doses of hope and hopelessness at unequal intervals. In view of the injustice in the world, we are rather justified in thinking first not of the penny all labourers received from the householder regardless of how many hours they had worked (Matt. 20:14), but of those who arrived last only to take everything away and leave. They may have left to go shopping for the preparation of a "memorable celebration" of Christmas! They are ones who inhabit houses that were built by another. They have eaten what was planted by somebody else (cf. Isa. 65:22). How far are they from those that are "given grace according to the measure of the gift of Christ" (Eph. 4:7)? How far are they from that wealth of grace that is abundantly given without distinction "for the edifying of the body of Christ" (Eph. 20:12)? We are facing a reality, which has different levels and perspectives. In our days, Basil the Great's meditation on "I will pull down my barns" (Luke 12:18) retains its value: "The bread that you hide belongs to the hungry, the garment that you keep in the storehouse belongs to the naked one, the shoes that you do not need belong to the barefooted... You do wrong to all those whom you could help."[1] No matter how many different forms of property we may have today compared with the 4th century of our era, the issue has always been the plague of selfishness and indifference towards the needs of others, which leaves no room for love. This is why the same father of the church addressing a rich man says: "the more wealth you possess the less love you display."[2]

As we experience and remember our reality, we look and pray for that "new earth" (Isa. 65:17) which was created for those who "shall plant vineyards, and eat the fruit of them" (Isa. 65:21). Today our inner eyes look, together with the eyes of previous generations, together with the eyes of the prophet, for those signs of a transformed reality that combines liberation from sin, the renewing presence of the living Lord, the end of the world of hopelessness, eternity... When high and fierce waves come, many will unfortunately pass away, many will lose their loved ones, many will despair. However, life and hope will not vanish altogether.

There will always be eyes wide open to see, beyond tribulations, the unmistakable signs of the presence of the One who has conquered the world and invites us not to lose hope (cf. John 16:33). It is in this world that signs of sanctity shine to announce the kingdom of heaven. There may be an eschatological dimension in the expectation of coming "to the measure of the stature of the fullness of Christ" (Eph. 4:13), but the church has always declared that there are among us those who reveal the image of God in their person without the mask fostered in the laboratory of this world. We do not despise this world, but its machinery, which causes "the voice of weeping... the voice of crying" (Isa. 65:19). We despise the mentality that contradicts the will of God. We need and cherish those who of their own free will do care about "hunger and thirst after righteousness" (Matt. 5:6) thus making manifest the kingdom in the world.

Hunger in the world constitutes a problem both spiritual and economic. The problem of justice in the world is placed first at the level of the human person. Every individual's wisdom, discretion or clear-sightedness is important in order to confront injustice, which causes immense problems and explosive situations in society. Economic inequality is not an evil as such, because it can prove to be a source of feelings of charity and solidarity, and a step towards moral progress. According to St Clement of Alexandria, wealthy people are blessed when they share their possessions with others.[3]

Beyond individual responsibility, there is an urgent need for a collective and global effort to address and overcome as many existent social problems as possible. Globalization and technological progress require ever wider cooperation among as many agencies as possible, especially those which are more advanced in infrastructure and specialists. This effort seems not to be effective (in the sense of sustainable solutions) within the context of industrial associations of organized interests (either business cartels or trade unions or corporate groups etc.). These bodies seem to be motivated by the spirit of material profit and to vindicate the rights of special interest groups. Activists in these associations may have zeal, but not that knowledge of which St Paul speaks in his letter to the Romans.

In Romans 10:3 Paul seems to address zealots of all times: "They, being ignorant of God's righteousness and going about to establish their own righteousness, have not submitted themselves unto the righteousness of God." It is not that zeal is necessarily irrelevant or disastrous. The problem arises when zeal manifests human freedom to the point of opposing God's goodness and righteousness, to the point of turning one's eye evil when facing goodness (cf. Matt. 20:15), to the point of contesting God's will to offer his grace in whatever way or circumstance

He chooses. Zeal retains its value as an endeavour to act positively in society. However, our zealous acts can never be the guarantee of justice, because justice will always be a gift of grace. We seek that supreme gift when we take all our worldly tribulations and preoccupations to the altar to celebrate the holy eucharist, where the material world is changed into the divine reality of a new heaven and a new earth.

Taking this gift into the world, we are called to be celebrants of the liturgy after the liturgy, not as activists but primarily as Christ-bearers "in spirit and in truth" (John 4:24). Manifesting the gift of grace to the world we count not on any human power but on our faith in Jesus Christ. In the words of St Paul "we have believed in Jesus Christ, that we might be justified by the faith of Christ, and not by the works of the law" (Gal. 2:16). This faith is accompanied by hope, the hope that awaits the fulfilment of all. Faith without hope will end up in mere formality; it will not be the manifestation of life.

If industrial associations and bodies of organized interests (as above) seem to be inadequate to organize the efforts needed to overcome social problems in the spirit of the gospel, this does not mean that collective or global efforts are doomed. Christians are called upon to face their problems in the light of the body of Christ risen from the dead "endeavouring to keep the unity of the Spirit in the bond of peace" (Eph. 4:3). We cannot keep silent in view of the fact that Christian divisions are a reminder of weakness, which in our world entails the inability to confess one body, one Spirit, one Lord, one faith, one baptism, one God and Father of all (cf. Eph. 4:4-6). If weakness is part of our reality, it is a fact that weakness alone cannot undermine faith accompanied by Christian hope.

What really threatens faith and hope is indifference or selfish activity in life. In a globalized world Christians are called more urgently than ever to cooperate and learn to act together with trust in God and in each other. It is a calling, which aims not only at Christian unity but at the unity of all humankind. In the prospect of this unity, men and women of faith have a chance to act in solidarity with the weak and poor, thus giving new life to their faith. This horizontal extension of human activity in any case will need to be fed by the vertical relation with God the Father who pours out his grace through Jesus Christ in the communion of the Holy Spirit.

NOTES

[1] 7, PG31, 276C-277A.
[2] 1, PG31, 281B.
[3] Pedagogue 3,6,35,5.

"We Are One"

BISHOP DR YEZNIK PETROSSIAN

Truly I perceive that God shows no partiality but in every nation any one who fears him and does what is right is acceptable to him.

(Acts 10:34-36)

Dear brothers and sisters in Christ,

I greet you all in the name of our Lord and pray for a successful outcome and prayerful deliberations for our inter-Orthodox meeting.

Today we have scriptural readings and a theme for meditation: prophecy of Joel (3:1-11), Acts of the Apostles (10:9-35) and the gospel of Matthew (15:21-28).

Before making any reflections on the topic of this day, once again I would like to recall the events that happened weeks ago, at the end of the passing year, when more than one hundred and sixty thousand innocent people became victims of a natural disaster.

We remember these people with respect and honour their memory. Let us remember them in our silent prayers for a moment.

Believing that we have been called to overcome the violence in the world and work for the establishment of justice, peace and harmony, I recall the verses from the Acts of Apostles. "Truly I perceive that God shows no partiality but in every nation any one who fears him and does what is right is acceptable to him" (Acts 10:34-36).

This verse leads me into the multicultural world of ancient Palestine of the first-century Roman empire. Their relations are matters of discussion. How are the cultural diversities seen in the light of the new faith that Jesus brought with him? How do these cultural diversities affect the religious life and beliefs of the faithful?

These questions concern us even today. How do we face our cultural diversities and how do we cope with the reality of our differences? As it was in the early church, today also Christianity is diverse and our cultural diversities affect our religious life.

Believing in the verses of today's scripture readings, and especially those of Matthew and Acts, I would say that our Lord does not recognize limits and boundaries. This is a fact that can be neither denied nor ignored. This is what our common study of the Bible shows and teaches.

In this regard I also want to recall what Jesus told the robber who said, "Lord, remember me when you come into your kingdom." And Jesus answered, "Truly I tell you, today you will be with me in paradise" (Luke 23:43).

There was diversity in the early church and our fathers coped with it, believing that this kind of diversity comprised the beauty of the church. This is a diversity that we have inherited. It is a fact that Jesus Christ has revealed himself through different cultures during history.

We read the Bible and understand it according to our cultural and confessional inheritance, according to our background and personal conviction, but yet we are one. And this is the key of the mystery, since we are one because we have Jesus Christ. We are one because we are sons and daughters of our God. We are one because we believe in the Risen God and Jesus who has come for all the people and for the whole creation.

We have to confess that besides our cultural differences there are also human factors that in the course of history have become reasons for misunderstandings and objections, mistrust and prejudices.

These human factors, which had deprived us of the joyous communion, today are also challenging us in the present ecumenical world.

We are struggling for unity and harmony, love and respect, yet there are obstacles preventing us from accepting each other.

The questions of ecumenical openness and collaboration on local levels still remain unanswered. As someone coming from a former communist country, I cannot accept this view without objection and fear. This is the dominance of one polar world and one-sided pressure on Orthodox countries. This is the lack of trust and mutual understanding, one-sided aggressive mission by new religious movements and massive injustice in the field of Christian missions.

These are also examples which, in my opinion, do not fit to the theme of today's readings. We represent Orthodox churches, churches which are sometimes considered as conservative. However, I would say that these are a community and communion of churches who have preserved the old and ancient but living faith in Jesus Christ. This is a treasure that we have gained by the blood of our martyrs and living witnesses.

This is our faith that we have inherited from our pious fathers, who were not only steadfast to preserve their faith and follow the teaching of the gospel, but also were aware of the imperative of preserving our identities and spiritual entities in the face of historical upheavals and pressures.

We were victimized, marginalized, killed and deprived, but still we preserve what Jesus told us and what is the highest commandment of Jesus Christ: "In everything do to others as you would have them do to you" (Matt. 7:12).

I think that in our ecumenical gatherings we perhaps have to study carefully the words of the apostle Paul in his first letter addressed to the community of the Corinthian church:

> Consider your own call, brethren; not many of you were wise by human standards, not many were powerful, not many were of noble birth. But God chose what is foolish in the world to shame the wise; God chose what is weak in the world to shame

the strong; God chose what is low and despised in the world, things that are not, to reduce to nothing things that are, so that no one might boast in the presence of God. He is the source of your life in Christ Jesus, who became for us wisdom from God, and righteousness and sanctification and redemption, in order that, as it is written, "Let the one who boasts, boast in the Lord" (1 Cor. 1:26-31).

With these reflections I pray to God to strengthen us in our mission, because He is the most blessed with the Son and the Holy Spirit unto the ages of ages. Amen.

"You Shall Love the Lord Your God…"

METROPOLITAN ANBA BISHOY OF DAMIETTE

Now Jesus sat opposite the treasury and saw how the people put money into the treasury. And many who were rich put in much. Then one poor widow came and threw in two mites, which make a quadrans. So He called his disciples to himself and said to them, "Assuredly, I say to you that this poor widow has put in more than all those who have given to the treasury; for they all put in out of their abundance, but she out of her poverty put in all that she had, her whole livelihood."

(Mark 12:41-44 NKJ)

The questions that might come to mind on reading this moving narrative are:

- How could a poor widow donate to the treasury of the Lord's house when she is in need of assistance?
- How could she offer *all that she had, her whole livelihood*; the law only required her to give the tithe (10 percent)?
- Why did Christ the Lord consent to this widow's action, allowing her to depart having no provisions, being poor and widowed?
- Why did He not order his disciples to give her monetary assistance, now that she had nothing, having "put in *all that she had, her whole livelihood*"?

The story started this way:

Now Jesus sat opposite the treasury and saw how the people put money into the treasury. And many who were rich put in much. Then one poor widow came and threw in two mites, which make a quadrans.

(Mark 12:41-42)

Christ the Lord wanted to alert his disciples to a lesson in offering, giving them an idea of his standards, which differ from general human standards.

He wanted them to understand that in his viewpoint the value of a person's act is not based on the size of this act, but on the person's feelings and intentions behind the action; any virtue without love and humility is not accounted a virtue before God.

No doubt this widow's heart was filled with love for God, therefore she gave *all that she had, her whole livelihood*, literally living the commandment: "You shall love the LORD your God with all your heart, with all your soul, and with all your mind" (Matt. 22:37).

In her humility she was not ashamed to present an extremely meagre amount amid the wealthy who possessed much and presented abundantly. She exposed herself to derision and ridicule by others because the force of her love made her offer what she had, even if it appeared minimal in the eyes of others.

This woman sincerely lived the commandment despite her personal circumstances. Despite her extreme poverty she wanted to receive the blessing of giving and offering the tithes. But what could her tithes amount to? Perhaps there was no coinage equivalent to one-tenth of two mites, but even if there were, she wanted to present reverence to the Lord of Hosts which surpassed the limits of giving, the tithes... therefore she "put in *all that she had, her whole livelihood*", while the tongue of her heart said, "Accept O Lord my humble offering which does not befit your magnificence... but, this is all I have."

This woman's contribution was very great in the sight of the Lord, therefore He did not object or prevent her, nor did He hurt her feelings by giving her charity at this specific point in time.

The angels praised with the praises of blessing; the scene was so outstanding that it moved heaven, just as Jacob's ladder was thronged by his pure angel ascending and descending. This wondrous scene was recorded in the holy Bible as a moral lesson to the church throughout all generations.

It was a love sonnet delighting Christ the Lord's heart, to which He wanted to direct his disciples' attention, so they would stand in bewilderment at this awesome scene, which was magnified and glorified by his presence.

The poor widow went away in all the reverence of holiness, surrounded by legions of angels who were won by this widow's love and humility.

This poor widow who was rich in love and humility symbolizes the church which was widowed after being expelled from paradise, to whom the Lord spoke through the mouth of Isaiah the prophet saying:

> "Do not fear, for you will not be ashamed; neither be disgraced, for you will not be put to shame; for you will forget the shame of your youth, and will not remember the reproach of your widowhood any more. For your Maker is your husband, the Lord of hosts is his name; and your Redeemer is the Holy One of Israel; He is called the God of the whole earth. For the Lord has called you like a woman forsaken and grieved in spirit, like a youthful wife when you were refused," says your God. "For a mere moment I have forsaken you, but with great mercies I will gather you. With a little wrath I hid my face from you for a moment; but with everlasting kindness I will have mercy on you," says the Lord, your Redeemer.
>
> *(Isa. 54:4-8)*

No doubt the Lord greatly provided for this poor widow after she left the temple, personally supplying her care after she offered him *all that she had, her whole livelihood*.

Likewise the church, through the Virgin St Mary, offered in full love and humility *all that she had*, a rational human body and spirit. The Lord took a perfect humanity from the Virgin Mary with which He entered into a new covenant with humanity. This human body and spirit which the Lord took is symbolized by this widow's two mites, which bear the greatest value in the Lord's eyes, "more than all those who have given to the treasury".

Likewise, we hear the Lord recite this poetic sonnet through the mouth of Isaiah the prophet:

> O you afflicted one, tossed with tempest, and not comforted, behold, I will lay your stones with colourful gems, and lay your foundations with sapphires. I will make your pinnacles of rubies, your gates of crystal, and all your walls of precious stones. All your children shall be taught by the Lord, and great shall be the peace of your children.
>
> *(Isa. 54:11-13)*

After the Lord's birth from the Virgin Mary by the work of the Holy Spirit, Christ the Lord became *all that she had, her whole livelihood.* Not only to St Mary, but also to the whole church, Christ the Lord was himself *all that she had, her whole livelihood.*

The day of redemption came and the Virgin Mary willingly offered her only-begotten Son (humanly) to the cross, and the church offered *all that she had, her whole livelihood* into the Lord's treasury… and the Lord accepted humanity's gift to him… which is simultaneously the Father's gift to humanity… it was the greatest gift… it was Jacob's ladder… and it was the Father's pleasure.

On the Way to Christian Unity

REV. DR PROF. IOAN SAUCA

Be of the same mind, having the same love, being in full accord and of one mind. Do nothing from selfish ambition or conceit, but in humility regard others as better than yourselves. Let each of you look not to your own interests, but to the interests of others. Let the same mind be in you that was in Christ Jesus...

(Phil. 2:2-5)

But whoever wishes to become great among you must be your servant, and whoever wishes to be first among you must be slave of all.

(Mark 10:43-44)

The two texts from Philippians 2:1-11 and Mark 10:32-45 are to be read and reflected upon in the Bible study groups on the day when the major topic of the discussion in the assembly plenary will be the unity of the church. Reading carefully those two texts, one may ask what could be the relation between these and the concern for unity. Is there any relation at all?

Though the content of those two texts does not refer directly to the nature of the unity of the church we seek, it refers to the process, or rather to the attitude one may adopt during the process of common search for Christian unity.

The key words arising from the two texts are so familiar to Orthodox theology and spirituality: humility, love, service and care for others.

Though the search for unity remains a commitment for all those involved in ecumenical encounters and dialogue, the difficulties persist as different parties understand and approach it differently. For some, the dialogue is accepted as long as the different identities, as they are understood and lived in their historical developments, are not threatened. There is a fear of losing one's particularity; there is a fear that in the process of searching for unity, some may gain and some may lose. And no one wants to be a loser.

There is, at times, a power struggle of offering one's "truth" over against the "truths" of the others. For the people with such thinking, attitudes and approaches, the dialogue is accepted and promoted as long as it leads to and remains at the level of "cooperation", but does not imply any notion of change or transformation.

The problem is that some of us behave, at times, as the two disciples from the gospel text of the day. They asked to be put on the right and left hand of Jesus when He will come in his kingdom. However, some of us involved in the ecumenical dialogues and in search for Christian unity behave as being already placed at the right and left hand of Jesus. And from there we speak arrogantly to the others.

Christian truth is not an ideology; it is not a system of thought, a collection of right formulations in conflict or competition with other ideological systems. The Christian truth is to be found in the person of Christ who offered himself as being the truth, the way and the life. The Christian witness refers to the witness of the fullness of Christ. Through Christ, we have relation to the Father and are partakers of the koinonia of the Holy Spirit. The formulations of the early ecumenical councils were not innovations or additions or further doctrinal developments of the apostolic kerygma, but affirmations and articulations about the fullness of Christ when it was challenged or disputed. Even then, it was not the intent of clearly putting in antagonism the bad and the good verbal formulations. The main reason for such formulations was related to the issue of salvation, which was very much dependent on the fullness of life in Christ.

The dialogue with the Oriental Orthodox churches and the final signed theological agreement show once more that what matters in the end is the content of the fullness of the apostolic faith and not necessarily its historically conditioned formulation. Yet, the witness to the integrity of apostolic faith is important since it is a precondition of a right and full relationship with Christ. And for this reason, the Orthodox are constantly reminding the ecumenical movement about the importance of the witness to apostolic faith today in the process of the search for Christian unity.

The affirmation of the apostolic faith, however, does not save automatically. It has to be appropriated and lived in one's life. It is interesting that the first Christians were called as those who belonged to the way (*Tes odou ontas,* Acts 9:2). Christianity is a way of life, the life in Christ, a holistic life which refers to human integrity, soul and body, and in its relation to the whole of creation. That fullness of life is leading to *theosis*, to the measure of the full stature in Christ (Eph. 4:13).

Theosis is a process, not a static event. It goes from one degree to another, being transformed from one degree of glory to another (2 Cor. 3:17). The process starts here and now but continues in eternity for those who will live in God's kingdom (*epectasis*). It is also interesting that the last judgement does not consist of an examination of the knowledge of the right theological formulations, but on the extent to which one has lived out that theology in communion with God through Christ in the Holy Spirit (Matt. 25).

The *sine qua non* for efficiency in ecumenical dialogues and in the process of advancing towards the visible unity of Christians is *humility*. There is a need to accept and acknowledge that no one is self-sufficient and everyone needs the others in order to successfully confront the common challenges of our times.

It is normal that in the process of dialogue everyone comes with his/her identity, convinced that the integrity of apostolic faith is being witnessed to within the framework of his/her own confession. In the process of dialogue, while we all struggle to witness to the integrity of apostolic faith, such a witness should be done with humility and with careful listening to the others. Among the masterpieces of the Orthodox pioneers of the modern ecumenical movement – such as the encyclical letter of the Ecumenical Patriarchate in 1920, or the statement on the unity of the church elaborated at the New Delhi assembly (the two pillars of the Orthodox participation in the ecumenical movement) – show no sign of arrogance or self-sufficiency. They are rather a humble attempt to place the Orthodox churches within Christ's concern and wish for the unity of all, and "doing the truth", as it has been witnessed by the whole church in each place and time, and is being witnessed to with much love and humility.

In such an encounter and dialogue, the Orthodox have and could still offer much from the common treasury of the early church, in the attempt to find the common basis of Christian unity. The faith of the apostles is not a matter of negotiation or relativization, and the unity we seek is absolutely against such possible practices. But in a dialogue, one cannot only speak; it has also to listen. God has given so many gifts to the others in the course of history; there is a long experience in living out the Christian faith in contexts which were unknown to the Orthodox before but which confront them today. In the search for the unity we seek, the Orthodox should learn to listen as well and to learn from the others. As long as the apostolic faith is safeguarded and witnessed to, the unity cannot be monolithic or one-sided; it is always polyphonic. The unity we seek has as its basis the trinitarian existence who is oneness out of many; the body of Christ who is one but out of many members; and the Holy Spirit which is one, but with many and diverse gifts.

Moving Towards the Assembly and Beyond

Ecclesiological Implications and Challenges
of the Special Commission Report and Proposals

METROPOLITAN ANBA BISHOY OF DAMIETTE

Looking towards the future of the ecumenical movement invites us to examine the increasing need of the world today for Christian witness, and to try our best to bring the World Council of Churches to the status of being an active tool in this respect.

"More than 50 years of being together should not be lost but fed into future proposals for the ecumenical movement."[1] Much has been learned in these years and the churches have been enriched by sharing together in their journey towards common Christian witness in order to transform the world.

The question before us today is to what extent are we able to listen to each other without being obliged to compromise our self-understanding of the church? Are we able to reach a point of dialogue without being afraid of a burning issue which would involve parliamentary decision-making procedures?

The last meeting of the Steering Committee of the Special Commission on Orthodox Participation in the WCC, in Minsk, Belarus, 16-19 June 2004, stated in its report:

> The Committee underlined that the new methodology of consensus, based on deliberation and discernment, is a move to a new ethos and culture requiring a change of attitudes. This shift has the potential to strengthen and deepen the fellowship of churches. (item 3 of the report on consensus)

Without this new ethos and culture, it is very difficult for the Orthodox to continue their journey of membership in the WCC, since they feel that the programmes and the reports issued during the meetings of the Council, whether in governing bodies or in other committees, are in many instances against their understanding of the church or their Orthodox traditions. Yet without the Orthodox the WCC would become merely a pan-Protestant council.

While the Orthodox have been deeply committed to the ecumenical movement since the beginning, nevertheless they have been greatly disappointed by feeling that they were always defeated through parliamentary acts in the proceedings of the Council.

As we move towards the ninth assembly, scheduled for 2006 in Porto Alegre, Brazil, we are carrying with us – as Orthodox – great hopes for the future of the ecumenical movement, and for a clear understanding by other confessional groups in the Council.

The Orthodox never seek to have the upper hand in the Council, since this would imply a pan-Orthodox council, and this they can convene outside the WCC.

In his preface to the issue of *The Ecumenical Review* devoted to the final report of the Special Commission on Orthodox Participation in the WCC, Rev. Dr Konrad Raiser, then general secretary of the WCC, in accordance with this view, wrote: [2]

> Contrary to the implications of some criticisms of the World Council following the reception of the Special Commission's report, the action adopted by the central committee is by no means a matter of either Orthodox or Protestant churches gaining an upper hand. On the contrary, never before have the WCC and its member churches faced up to the fundamental issues of membership so seriously or honestly. We look forward to continuing dialogue in that spirit. The Special Commission has initiated a process that could lead to a change in our institutional culture, to extension of the ecumenical table, to improvement in the way Christian churches relate with one another and, finally, to renewal in their witness and ministry to a world torn by division, suspicion and violence.

In the same line Rev. Dr Heinz-Joachim Held of the Evangelical Church in Germany, former moderator of the WCC's central committee, wrote the following – before the central committee had taken action: [3]

> It is clear from the final report of the Commission that there has been, probably for the first time in the history of the WCC, a thorough, patient but also frank and constructive debate between the Orthodox and the Protestant ecumenical ethos within the WCC. At the same time, there is every sign that there has been a serious, genuine and far-reaching review process that points to ways in which the WCC can move beyond its historically Protestant original influences to become an organ of the ecumenical movement, an organ which intrinsically acts and thinks in a way which also gives rights and space to other confessional identities. It would then become more ecumenical than it has been able to be until now. I think this is a genuine opportunity. I would like to congratulate the Special Commission for its work and its results and I can only hope that in discussing this report the central committee of the WCC will take the time to try and understand what it is about and make decisions along the lines being proposed.

A plus for the WCC on the way into the future

I am convinced that we are dealing with a historic moment in the life of the WCC, a "kairos" time, which the WCC must clearly recognize and discern with spiritual authority. I would like to outline its significance through the following theses:

- It is at long last taking Orthodox member churches seriously.
- It has accepted the long overdue consequences of their many years of membership, which for some Orthodox churches dates back to the foundation of the WCC.

- Critical Orthodox "demands" are not only widely understood by many other member churches but in some respects also shared.
- These other member churches will be able to gain much theologically and ecclesiologically for their own ecumenical vision from the participation of Orthodox churches on the basis of "parity".
- The WCC will in the end be internally strengthened through the (self) critical reception of the experiences of its first fifty years and through the careful implementation of the proposals of the Special Commission. It will have a renewed conviction in its original tasks and thus strengthened can approach the next fifty years of its history.

Furthermore, the final report seems to me to be a sign that it is worthwhile to have ongoing, thorough and comprehensive work in commissions, and that such fundamental questions cannot be dealt with at the market of opinions in larger assemblies held in public. It is much better to handle these questions by creating a long-term fellowship of life, work and prayer with experienced and authorized delegates who can meet – albeit occasionally – over a number of years, and who can get to know each other at a personal level and come to a level of spiritual trust. The understanding and reception of the Special Commission report at the WCC's ninth assembly is of crucial importance to the future of the ecumenical movement.

The Permanent Committee on Consensus and Collaboration is expected to play an important role in the life of the WCC. This Committee will, in the future, continue the work and concerns of the Special Commission after the ninth assembly.

The Steering Commission of the Special Commission in its Minsk report

affirmed that the mandate and terms of the Permanent Committee provide the necessary guarantee that it will continue "the authority, mandate, concerns and dynamic of the Special Commission" on Orthodox participation in the WCC.

It should be noted that the Permanent Committee would be a parity committee with half of its members being Orthodox.

Moreover, the Orthodox are called at every WCC meeting to have their own gatherings in order to coordinate their ways of participation in the life of the Council, and to present positive contributions during this participation. They should have enough courage to discuss burning issues without fear, since they are called to witness biblical truth. But they should first be united in one mind together.

We would like to take this opportunity to congratulate the new general secretary of the WCC, Rev. Dr Samuel Kobia, on his election and his contribution to the work of the Special Commission, as expressed in his address to the meeting of its Steering Committee in Minsk, June 2004, when he underlined that, "although he had not been personally involved in the work of the Special Commission, he had followed the developments carefully. He emphasized his commitment to ensuring the implementation of the recommendations of the Special Commission.

"He invited the [Steering Committee] to think about the period ahead as the WCC prepares for the ninth assembly and looks beyond, and proposed some areas where the experience gained from the Special Commission could be of particular help (e.g. membership contributions; reconfiguration of the ecumenical movement; ecumenical space, spirituality)."

The Steering Committee "reviewed plans for a progressive introduction of a consensus methodology in WCC meetings. The proposals, to be tested during the WCC central committee in 2005, are designed to overcome the traditional divide between majority and minority votes, and to foster a new quality of collaboration." Rev. Dr Kobia linked consensus to a search for "spiritual discernment" which could strengthen WCC efforts in dialogue and advocacy. "Consensus opens the way to a new, more spiritual, culture for the WCC.[4]

The Orthodox are called to work hard in order to present a good example of the search for the unity of the churches by giving more attention to the outcome of the work of the Joint Commission on Theological Dialogue between the Orthodox Church and Oriental Orthodox Churches, where three official agreements were signed (1989 in Egypt, 1990 and 1993 in Switzerland), with the aim of the restoration of full communion between the two families of Orthodoxy. The second agreement states:

> In the light of our agreed statement on Christology as well as of the above common affirmations, we have now clearly understood that both families have always loyally maintained the same authentic Orthodox Christologcial faith, and the unbroken continuity of the apostolic tradition, though they may have used Christological terms in different ways. It is this common faith and continuous loyalty to the apostolic Tradition that should be the basis of our unity and communion.

The Joint Commission and its sub-committees are expected to continue their work after Metropolitan Emmanuel of France has been appointed as its co-chairman, substituting our beloved brother and great contributor Metropolitan Damaskinos of Switzerland, whom we shall always remember and pray for.

NOTES

[1]   Final Report of the Special Commission on Orthodox Participation in the WCC (Sec. A-II, 7. – Doc. No. Gen 5, p. 3).
[2]   Volume 55, Number 1, January 2003, p. 3.
[3]   *Ibid.*, pp. 57-58.
[4]   Press Update, WCC Media relations office, 23 June 2004.

Looking Towards the Future

Ecclesiological Implications and Challenges
of the Special Commission Report

DR PETER C. BOUTENEFF

The report of the Special Commission on Orthodox Participation in the WCC identifies

> two basic ecclesiological self-understandings, namely of those churches (such as the Orthodox) which identify themselves with the one, holy, catholic, and apostolic church, and those which see themselves as parts of the one, holy, catholic and apostolic church.

The report goes on to say that

> these two ecclesiological positions affect whether or not churches recognize each other's baptism as well as their ability or inability to recognize one another as churches. They also affect the way churches understand the goal of the ecumenical movement, its instruments – including the WCC and its foundational documents. [1]

This paragraph comes at the beginning of the Special Commission report, thus setting the stage for the report's observations and recommendations. It is a clear statement of what we have long been calling "the ecclesiological problem" of the ecumenical movement. It is a summary, albeit simplistic, of what makes the Orthodox churches theologically uneasy in their participation.

While rightly placing ecclesiological issues at the centre of things, the Special Commission does not say anything particularly new about ecclesiology. The Orthodox churches at the New Delhi assembly (1961) had already put it very clearly, in a simple, symmetrical sentence: "For the Orthodox, the Orthodox church is just the church." [2] We have been saying this all along, ever since the inaugural meeting of Faith and Order at Lausanne (1927), and in all the famous "separate statements" that Orthodox delegates have felt compelled to produce at landmark meetings. We identify ourselves, as a particular canonical and historical body, with the one, holy, catholic and apostolic church.

Although it has been necessary to articulate and rearticulate our ecclesiological identity in the ecumenical context, it appears that we have indeed been heard, in some contexts at least. During the work of the Special Commission, the other WCC member churches listened carefully to the Orthodox concerns of every kind, and had many occasions to hear of our ecclesiological self-understanding. It is only natural, therefore, that they should then ask us the following question, as they have in the Special Commission report: Is there space for other churches in Orthodox ecclesiology? How would this space and its limits be described?[3]

This question could be rephrased or elaborated in the following ways. If the Orthodox church is the church, what is the status of the non-Orthodox churches? Do they exist in an undifferentiated non-Orthodox and therefore non-ecclesiological void? Is there Christian life in the non-Orthodox churches? If there is a Christian pulse in at least some of the churches, do they share in some way the "space" occupied by the Orthodox church?

Regardless of how one answers it, it has to be said that this is a valid question. Indeed, it might have been asked with a great deal more exasperation: "You say you are the church, and we are not. We are heretics. Then why do you even bother with us?" Indeed, sometimes we hear it expressed in such ways. But the question was asked here in an honest and non-threatening way. We ought therefore to consider ourselves as being posed with a respectful and justified challenge. All the more, then, should this question occupy our attention. I believe it should pierce us.

The depth of the question

This question of the charismatic limits of the church depends upon how we define the church in the first place. And such a task may not be as straightforward as we might think. Unlike Christology and trinitarian theology, there is no unilaterally identifiable patristic ecclesiology. Fr Georges Florovsky consistently makes this observation:

> It is impossible to start with a formal definition of the church. For, strictly speaking, there is none which would claim any doctrinal authority. None can be found in the fathers. No definition has been given by the ecumenical councils.[4]

It is not that the fathers were silent about the church. When occasion warranted it, particularly in the face of particular schisms, important and authoritative treatises were written by the likes of St Cyprian of Carthage and St Augustine, not to mention the brief but critically important statements in the letters of St Ignatius of Antioch. But – especially compared to the church's Christological and trinitarian doctrine – we do not find anything approaching a comprehensive ecclesiology. Fr Alexander Schmemann sheds light on this reticence:

> In our own "sources" – the fathers, the councils, the liturgy – we do not find any formal definition of the church. This is not because of any lack of ecclesiological interest and consciousness, but because the church (in the Orthodox approach to her) does not exist (and therefore cannot be defined) apart from the very content of her life. The church, in other terms, is not an "essence" or "being" distinct from God, man, and the world, but is the very reality of Christ in us and us in Christ, a new mode of God's presence and action in his creation, of creation's life in God... Orthodox ecclesiology [therefore] is an attempt to present an icon of the church as life in Christ... For the church is an institution, but she is also a mystery, and it is mystery that gives meaning and life to institution and is, therefore, the object of ecclesiology.[5]

Yet as both Fr Florovsky and Fr Schmemann knew well from their own experience, the church in the 20th century lost the luxury of an ecclesiology based solely on mystery and apophasis. This was because the very fact of the new ecumenical encounter required of the Orthodox church an answer, both to its own constituency as well as to those outside, to the question of the limits of the church. If the church is, as Schmemann says, "the reality of Christ in us and us in Christ", is that reality actually inaccessible to those who are not members of the canonical Orthodox churches? And if it is accessible, then wherein lies the uniqueness of Orthodoxy?

The urgency of the question for us

Exploring the question of the limits of the church has never been simple, and it is particularly complex today. A fair number of essays exist on the subject at the hands of 20th-century thinkers (Bulgakov, Florovsky, Nissiotis, Clapsis, Tsypin, Zizioulas, Cavarnos and several others). Not only in writing, but in our practical approaches to other churches, we must be honest that the approaches to this question vary considerably both between and within our local churches. To put this more sharply: we must admit that we do not at present have a clear and consistent Orthodox position concerning the ecclesiological status of non-Orthodox Christians as a whole, or of particular non-Orthodox churches.

For some, especially (though not exclusively) within some of the groups whose chief raison d'être is "anti-ecumenism", there is no Christian life outside the Orthodox church, and one cannot speak of ecclesial, sacramental grace outside the canonical Orthodox church (however these groups might define "the canonical Orthodox church"). We also know that the practice of the reception of converts into the Orthodox church varies from place to place, and from decade to decade. Some accept all non-Orthodox into the Orthodox church by baptism (or "re-baptism"). Others distinguish between categories of non-Orthodox, and receive some by baptism, some by chrismation, and some simply by confession of faith.

While the Orthodox church has always enjoyed a unity that holds together a certain diversity of local practices, and sometimes even a diversity of certain theological positions, the range of ecclesiological approaches which we experience today is beyond the limits of a healthy diversity.

Our dividedness on this question fractures us. It does so because it is a question that is so central to our own being, and central to the context within which our church dwells. Our church abides in local expressions throughout the world, in settings that are increasingly pluralistic. There are few places remaining in the world where the Orthodox church is the sole expression of Christianity, and few places where Christianity is the sole expression of religious faith. So the Orthodox church must give an account of itself, and therefore, by extension, of that which exists outside itself.

So once again, not only because we owe other Christians an answer to it, but because we ourselves are divided by it – the question of the status of non-Orthodox churches must indeed occupy us, to the point of piercing us.

Beginnings of an answer

Is there space for other churches in Orthodox ecclesiology? How would that space and its limits be described?

In seeking an appropriate framework from which to approach the question, Orthodox participants in the ecumenical movement have often striven to call the other member churches to an awareness of the historical schisms and splits (which we can name and place in particular points in history) that led up to the divided Christendom that is evident to us today. Crucially, these divisions are understood as occurring not within the church (for the body of Christ cannot be divided) but from the church and from the apostolic tradition to which the Ortho-dox church bears a uniquely unbroken witness. Healing, then, is a return to that undivided historical church and its tradition.[6]

Seeing division and unity in this way can in principle be presented in a very stark fashion, as summarized by a series of airtight statements, each of which might logically follow upon the previous:

- There is no division in the church, only from the church.
- The Orthodox church is the church.
- Division from the canonical Orthodox church is therefore division from the church.
- Healing of division is return to the canonical Orthodox church.

There is a sense in which we Orthodox do indeed align ourselves with each of these statements. But taken as a whole, they may imply that there is only *one kind of division*, a decisive one which places one entirely outside the body of Christ. If that is the case, then anyone who is not a member of the Orthodox church, whether a Lutheran or an Anglican or a Muslim or a shaman, is equally estranged from the body of Christ, equally devoid of Christian life. But this is far from what our hearts tell us, and far as well from what history and Tradition tell us.

Let us look at some of the ways in which history, contemporary theologians and contemporary inter-Orthodox realities temper such a picture and point to possibilities for "space" in Orthodox ecclesiology.

Tradition and its contemporary interpretation

History – and in particular the history of schism – offers clues as to how we might reckon the ecclesial significance of non-Orthodox Christians. Here are a few examples, which are rather well known and often cited:

- We recall St Basil the Great, in his canonical epistle, who distinguishes three categories: heresies, schisms and "para-synagogues" or illegal congregations. Those whom he calls "heresies" are on the extreme end of the spectrum: they are Manichaeans, Valentinians, Marcionites and Montanists. On the other hand, those whom he calls "schismatic" are those whose separation has a remedy – and remarkably, he says they are still "of the church" (*ek tês ekkle-*

sias). They are not "the church", he does not even say they are "in the church", but they are of the church. It is not possible, of course, neatly and simply to apply St Basil's distinction in our own day, and imagine which of his three categories would apply to each of the virtually countless expressions of Christianity outside the Orthodox church.[7] Yet at the very least, St Basil urges us to differentiate between *different extents of separation*, some of which are anything but a severing from the body.

• Another favourite passage of those who seek insight into the church's treatment of schism comes from another of the great Cappadocian fathers, St Gregory the Theologian. In his funeral oration for St Athanasius the Great (Oration 21), he offers the image of a hand which draws up water out of a pool. He says that just as there are droplets of water trickling out through the fingers, "so also there is a separation between us and others, among whom are not only the impious, but also those who are most pious". As to these pious ones, some are separated due to "such doctrines that are of small consequence", and others as a result of "expressions intended to bear the same meaning," i.e. misunderstandings due to our use of terminology.

• As to the church's canonical discipline, we must note that the early church rejected the rigourist sects of Novatian and Donatus, of the 3rd and 4th centuries respectively, who sought to rebaptize the lapsed. Ever since then, the doctrine that recognizes the validity of sacraments *ex opere operato* is one of the bases for the church's tendency to recognize baptisms performed in "schismatic" churches.

Such examples from the early church have provided the ground for contemporary Orthodox theologians to begin reflecting on the question as it was posed through the ecumenical encounter. I will remind us of some examples, also familiar to us:

• Fr Georges Florovsky was one of the first to address the question explicitly, in his 1933 essay, "The Limits of the Church".[8] His conclusions in this essay are ground-breaking: speaking of Christians outside the Orthodox church as "schismatics", he says that while we may not properly say that they are "in the church", we would say that the church *continues to operate in the schisms*, in anticipation of their resolution. In those cases where we recognise baptism performed outside the Orthodox church, it is not a matter of oikonomia, since *oikonomia* can not make something out of nothing – it cannot magically fabricate sacramental grace where none existed. Therefore, where we do recognize non-Orthodox baptism it is a *de facto* recognition of a charismatic reality. Baptism outside the Orthodox church is not technically or dogmatically an entry into the church, in the same way that an Orthodox baptism is. But it is an entry into a Christian life, calling the believer to live in the light of Jesus Christ. (Within many Orthodox churches, persons entering the Orthodox church who had been baptized in the name of the Trinity and with water are typically not "re-baptized". This is not tantamount to recognising that they come from another "part" or "branch" of the body of

Christ, rather it confirms precisely what Florovsky elaborates in his essay, that the church "operates in the schisms.")

- Metropolitan John (Zizioulas) of Pergamon, working from an ontology that rests in the phenomenon of communion, and in turn upon a "koinonia ecclesiology", has been particularly sensitive to the question of koinonia outside the boundaries of Orthodoxy. In the face of questions about the nature of the WCC and the ecumenical movement, in the face of the justified caution of attributing to the WCC any ecclesiological character ("the WCC is not and must never become a super-church"),[9] Metropolitan John was bold and creative enough to speak of the WCC as having "ecclesiological significance". [10] For how else can one speak of a *de facto* fellowship of persons and groups of persons (dare we call them "churches"?) assembled in the name of Jesus Christ, to the glory of the One God, Father, Son, and Holy Spirit?[11] At any rate, Metropolitan John shows how we Orthodox ourselves implicitly suggest an ecclesiological significance to the Council, by calling for a theological basis to its existence (including, periodically, an insistence upon the inclusion of baptism as a criterion of membership). The more we insist upon a church-consciousness on the part of WCC member churches, and the more we insist on their theological integrity, e.g. through the conscious recitation of the Nicene Creed in the context of common prayer, the more we are testifying to our implicit conviction that there is something "of Christ", something "of the church" that is going on here.

Among Orthodox Christians today I do not believe that we could find a complete agreement on the above interpretations of traditional formulations and contemporary events. But these interpretations are useful nonetheless, for they suggest an entirely genuine irruption into the theoretical airtight image of the church. They suggest "space."

Orthodoxy today

The potential for "space", however imprecise and yet undefined, in Orthodox ecclesiology is suggested not only by historical episodes, patristic quotations, and the reflections of some contemporary theologians, but also in another way: by the life of our churches as they exist today. The relationships among and between our own churches raise questions which are not easy, but which are relevant to the question of our ecclesiological exclusivity or inclusivity.

As a fruitful beginning, let us consider the Chalcedonian-non-Chalcedonian divide, especially in light of the past forty years of rapprochement. It is not an exaggeration to say that our presence together as a common Orthodox witness in the face of the ecumenical movement, and our breakthroughs in the bilateral dialogues, have been among the most remarkable and joyous events in the history of the church. The unofficial and official dialogue process has featured many encouraging possibilities for the reunion of long-estranged families of Christians. But that process has also brought to light some very challenging questions related to unity and division:

- *Division from or within?* The official dialogues have been able to make the following remarkable statement about our two church families: "We have now clearly understood that both families have always loyally maintained the same authentic Orthodox Christological faith, and the unbroken continuity of the apostolic tradition." [12] Furthermore, local pastoral agreements, especially in Alexandria and Antioch, testify to a thorough sacramental recognition. What does this mean about the nature of division? Specifically, what does this mean regarding the principle that "there is no division within the church, only division *from* the church?" Was one of the families divided from the church? When each family considers its identity with the one holy church, does it "include" the other in that identification?
- *Oriental-Orthodox* unity. The period since the 1960s has witnessed a noteworthy and positive phenomenon: the effective formation of a church family. What is the nature of the ties that bind the Ethiopian, Coptic, Armenian, Syrian and Indian churches? How do each of these churches see themselves in relation to the one holy church? How does this church family see itself in relation to the one holy church? Does the question about "space for other churches" receive different answers among the churches of this family?
- *Eastern Orthodox unity.* What constitutes the unity and identity of the Orthodox church? To what extent does each local church maintain a consciousness of global Orthodoxy? How is Orthodox unity seen and served in Western Europe and America, where multiple parallel jurisdictions from different "mother churches" exist side by side? What is the ecclesiological status of the various churches and sects which are in schism from the canonical churches? In what specific ways does their status differ in our understanding from that of the non-Chalcedonian churches, from that of the Roman Catholic Church, and other churches?
- *Apostolic succession.* What does it mean if we acknowledge the apostolic succession not only of the two "families" (Orthodox and Oriental Orthodox), but also of the Roman Catholic Church, the Anglican churches, and certain Lutheran churches? What does this say about their "ecclesiological significance"?

Here again, opinions and practical implications concerning all of the above questions vary within all of our churches, but this does not make the challenges any less pointed, nor does it erase their relevance to the root question about the Orthodox unity and the boundaries of the church.

* * *

The Orthodox church is the church, from which there are indeed divisions. But is this all we can say? We can go on to make the famous statement "we know where the church is, but we do not know where it is *not*". That statement is an important start, more important than many people acknowledge. But does not our situation demand that we investigate whether it is possible to go further, to become more specific, to become more *cataphatic*? We may well not arrive at a perfect uniformity on this question, but we can certainly achieve a greater coherence in our response.

I suggest that it may be possible, for now, at least to decide together that we want to begin answering together these questions about the ecclesiological status of those outside our canonical boundaries. We can do this either on our own, summoned by one of our churches, or alternately we could work under the rubric of the Special Commission which most recently posed us the question. But let us establish that we do want to work together on this.

It will not be simple. But we trust each other, and more than this we trust the Holy Spirit to guide us into all truth (John 16:13). We owe it not only to those outside the Orthodox Church, who have now formally put the question before us and await an answer, but also to ourselves.

NOTES

[1] Section B, paragraph 15.

[2] Response to the Statement on Unity, see online at http://www.wcc-coe.org/wcc/who/crete-02-e.html.

[3] Section B, paragraph 16.

[4] Collected Works, vol. 1 p. 57. See also vol 14 pp. 1 and 29.

[5] *St Vladimir's Theological Quarterly*, Vol. 11, No. 1, 1967, 35-39 (p. 35).

[6] I am not here talking about a theoretical "ancient undivided Church of the first millennium." That is a misleading formulation both because it implies that the present-day Church, unlike the ancient one, is "the *divided* Church," and also because it ignores ecclesiastical divisions that plagued the entire first millennium. The ancient undivided Church, for the Orthodox, is the Orthodox Church.

[7] Still, if one were to press further an application of St Basil's categories to the present day, it would be inappropriate to place today's Roman Catholics, Anglicans, and "mainline" Protestants (in terms of their official teachings) on a par with St Basil's Manichaeans, Gnostics and Montanists.

[8] *Church Quarterly Review*, 1933, available online at http://www.wcc-coe.org/wcc/who/crete-01-e.html. It is probable that Florovsky based his ideas on those of Fr Sergius Bulgakov, who published less widely known essays on the subject in the early 1930s. I note above some of the authors who have continued to explore the question.

[9] The Toronto Statement, 1950, III.i (see online at http://www.wcc-coe.org/wcc/who/morges-01-e.html).

[10] "The Self-understanding of the Orthodox and their Participation in the Ecumenical Movement", see online at http://www.wcc-coe.org/wcc/who/crete-04-e.html.

[11] Cf. the WCC Basis.

[12] Second Agreed Statement, Chambésy, 1990.

Introduction to Consensus [1]

MS ANNE GLYNN-MACKOUL

Potentially the most significant change to the World Council of Churches resulting from the work of the Special Commission on Orthodox Participation in the WCC – and certainly the most visible change – will be the shift in the process of making decisions from a parliamentary voting system that is based on "majority rule" for issues that find their way to the agenda of meetings, to a system designed to discern a consensus among delegates to the WCC about issues before the Council. Much work has been undertaken in preparation for this change and in February 2005 the central committee will embark upon its first experimental use of this new method. These brief comments will attempt to summarize how this juncture was reached and to explore some of the implications of this change for the Orthodox churches.

What is consensus decision-making?

The report of the Special Commission gives a very clear and concise definition of the process and in appendix B to the report, an elaboration of the reasons for the change.

a) The consensus method is a process for seeking the common mind of a meeting without deciding issues by means of voting. A consensus is reached when one of the following occurs:

   i) all are in agreement (unanimity);

   ii) most are in agreement and those who disagree are content that the discussion has been both full and fair and that the proposal expresses the general "mind of the meeting"; the minority therefore gives consent;

   iii) the meeting acknowledges that there are various opinions, and it is agreed that these be recorded in the body of the proposal (not just in the minutes);

   iv) it is agreed that the matter be postponed;

   v) it is agreed that no decision can be reached.

b) Therefore, consensus procedures allow any family of or other group of churches, through a spokesperson, to have their objections to any proposal addressed and satisfied prior to the adoption of the proposal. This implies that the family or group of churches can stop any proposal from passing until they have been satisfied that their concerns have been fully addressed.

c) Since consensus does not always involve unanimity, and since there will be rare cases when consensus procedures are tried and do not succeed, a mechanism will operate which allows the meeting to move forward to a decision. The revised rules of the WCC will need to specify how this mechanism works and to ensure that the consensus procedures are not weakened. This process of revision should include consultation with the Standing Committee.

d) Within a consensus model, minorities have a right for their reasoned opposition to a policy to be recorded, whether in the minutes, in reports of the meeting, or both, if they so request. [2]

Together with an acknowledgement that some matters will always need to be decided by voting, this is the basic framework for the consensus process. With the consent of the central committee, a process was set in motion to draft a rule to replace rule XVI that currently guides the conduct of meetings. The committees that have undertaken this work were designated according to the parity model of the Special Commission with half membership from Orthodox churches and half from other WCC member churches. Their work has been reported to the governing bodies of the Council and the Permanent Committee on Consensus and Collaboration, that is, the Standing Committee referenced in the report that continues the work of the Special Commission.

Why did the Special Commission recommend this change?

From the formation of the WCC, its meetings have been organized around a parliamentary process familiar to some of the churches in the West and to other secular and governmental organizations and bodies. Parliamentary procedures – sometimes referred to as "Robert's Rules of Order" – provide an efficient and usually orderly way of moving through a crowded agenda with a formal process of motions, amendments, debate and voting on matters that come before a meeting. But there are drawbacks to this model. Issues are engaged in an adversarial framework with debate "for and against" an issue, with voting "for and against" an issue; the majority is privileged, those who know well how to use the rules are privileged, and use of parliamentary procedures can become confrontational and be manipulated. In close decisions, a large proportion of those participating in the meeting can be left disgruntled even though the majority has prevailed, with potentially less than wholehearted support for implementing the decision. Where a persistent or institutional minority finds itself often on the "losing" side of votes, a sense of lack of ownership or of being disenfranchised can poison the atmosphere.

All of this, of course, at different times has marked the interaction of the Orthodox churches with the WCC. As is well known, the Orthodox churches are an institutional minority in the Council. Of the 342 current member churches, fewer than 25 percent are Orthodox churches. The Orthodox churches are assured of approximately 25 percent of seats on the central committee by agreement because of the size and structure of our churches, but of course, this still very significantly is a minority. Historically, the participation of Orthodox churches in the WCC has been marked by preparation of minority statements, distancing the Orthodox from decisions taken by the majority of WCC churches.

Comprehensive review of the results of the Special Commission reveals other recommendations as well. Even without implementation of some of the other recommended changes, such as to membership, the shift to consensus procedures has the potential to eliminate this persistent problem of the minority position of the Orthodox churches. However, the change is fundamentally not just a shift in the balance of power from favouring the Protestant churches of the North to favouring the Orthodox churches, as some anticipate. In fact, if the change is fully embraced by member churches, it has the possibility of radically changing the face and ethos of the Council in a way that will challenge and may inspire all of us as well as those to whom we speak.

Theological basis for the change to consensus discernment for the conduct of meetings

The World Council of Churches is not an organization like other organizations. It is a "fellowship of churches which confess the Lord Jesus Christ as God and Saviour according to the scriptures and therefore seek to fulfil together their common calling to the glory of the one God, Father, Son and Holy Spirit".[3] Writing in support of the change to consensus discernment as a method of conducting meetings, former WCC general secretary, the Rev. Dr Konrad Raiser, noted,

> All churches believe in the centrality of holy scripture in their life and doctrine. A significant image of the church in the New Testament is the image of the body of Christ, diverse yet one. In the life of the WCC, with its fundamental aim of promoting unity of all Christians, there must similarly be respect for diversity and difference. The rules and procedures that govern the Council should reflect this respect. By assuring that decisions taken by the Council reflect a consensus of those participating in the process, the Council models respect for one another, unity in diversity, and Christian fellowship.[4]

Scripture itself illumines the way towards this model. In the appendix to the report of the Special Commission, the authors stated

> it is arguable that the church, being the body of Christ, is true to its inner nature when it is exploratory, seeking the mind of Christ and striving after a consensus which can declare: "it seemed good to the Holy Spirit and to us" (Acts 15:28). Rather than striving to succeed in debate, our aim should be mutual submission, seeking to "understand what the will of the Lord is".
>
> *(Eph. 5:17)*

Eden Grace, a member of the WCC central committee, of the Special Commission and representative of the Society of Friends (Quakers), introduced a report of the work of the Special Commission on this topic with the following observation: "How we make decisions matters, because how we treat each other testifies to whether we are living in the Spirit or not." She offered the following scriptural foundation to conducting meetings in such a way that a body opens itself to the possibility of discerning the will of God:

> There are many... models of consensus-building, and no one right way to do it. But as Christians we share some basic principles that undergird our efforts. In 1 Corinthians 2:16, Paul tells us that, as a community, "We have the mind of Christ". This is a rather extraordinary claim! Christ is resurrected and present in our community, as our leader, and our decisions can be guided by his mind. Paul says more in Philippians 2:2-4 about the marks of Christ's mind in the community: "Be of the same mind, having the same love, being in full accord and of one mind. Do nothing from selfish ambition or conceit, but in humility regard others as better than yourselves. Let each of you look not to your own interests but to the interests of others. Let the same mind be in you that was in Christ Jesus." In 1 Corinthians 1:10, he exhorts the community, "Now I appeal to you, brothers and sisters, by the name of our Lord Jesus Christ, that all of you be in agreement, and that there be no divisions among you, but that you be united in the same mind and the same purpose."

Eden Grace concludes:

> It seems clear that, for Paul, the Christian community is characterized by a certain quality of relationship among its members, which develops as a consequence of faithful discernment of the presence of Christ. This quality he summarizes as unity. [5]

There is a palpable excitement growing among some delegates to the WCC to embark on this new process, particularly among delegates of churches who have seen or experienced the changes that have occurred in other settings where meetings are conducted according to a process of discernment – for example, the Uniting Church in Australia, the Presbyterian Church of Aotearoa New Zealand, the Canadian Council of Churches. This excitement anticipates the rich spiritual benefits of the change in process and the implications it holds that churches who have agreed to this are signalling their intention to deepen their commitment to one another and to the ecumenical movement. They are looking to us, the Orthodox churches, finally to engage fully in the Council, to bring to the work of the Council the riches of our spiritual heritage and tradition, now that the perennial source of our wariness will have been left behind.

Some concerns

But there are sceptics. There are sceptics within us, among our friends and even among those who most hope for the best possible outcome of this change. Dr Janice Love, a member of the Special Commission and of the sub-committee that offered consensus as a recommendation who has served as chair of the consensus rules drafting committee, pointed out in an article on consensus, "Orthodox members of the Special Commission also stated repeatedly that their goal in advocating consensus is primarily practical. They consider themselves to be a permanent minority and feel acutely the danger of being victimized by the tyranny of the majority."[6] Eden Grace's excellent paper, while celebrating this decision and hopeful for the future, includes a realistic assessment of "some of the fears that can be provoked as a body moves towards discernment-based decision-making". Among them is this observation:

> It is easy to see how the powerful stand to lose something, but it is equally true that the historic "minority" or "victim" groups in the congregation also stand to lose something. There is a certain power in claiming to be oppressed… But a new process for the church, which seeks to listen to and respect all, and to make decisions which care for the well-being of all, will require that some people lay aside their victim identity. In the WCC, this is one of the hard things we face in the years ahead. Now that some member churches, which have for years been demanding a fairer process, have had their grievance addressed, they must be willing to give up that grievance and become fully participating members of the whole. It remains to be seen whether they are willing and able to do that![7]

The Orthodox representatives to the World Council of Churches may recognize ourselves in her description, and may ask ourselves:

> Are we willing to listen to and respect all who speak? Are we representatives of the Orthodox churches, we guardians of and witness to such a rich spiritual heritage, supporting the move to consensus discernment for practical reasons only – finally to realize (properly) increased power and influence in decisions of the WCC — and not for the deeply spiritual and profound reasons that undergird this process?

Surely we must be ready to lay aside these complaints that have been thoroughly aired and substantively addressed and move into the future. We have been challenged to fully engage in this journey with the rest of this fellowship of churches, trusting that this body can discern the will of God as it conducts it business. We have initiated this process; whether we fully engage in the spirit and spiritual logic of consensus discernment will reveal our commitment to the fellowship.

Consensus in practice

The draft rule corresponds very closely with the practical framework developed in the Special Commission. The drafting committee has taken the report, the appendix and comments from the central committee and executive committee and has attempted to integrate this theory with practice from existing examples of consensus rules. We are beholden to the folks from Australia who have so generously given of their time, wisdom and experience, and were most appreciative of the careful review by the Evangelical Church in Germany whose comments were integrated into the work, as were the very detailed comments of the Steering Committee. We will try out the results of that work during the central committee in a limited setting with an opportunity to fine-tune the process.

During an assembly, meetings of the central committee and executive committee, decisions are made in all of the various aspects of the work, or business, of the Council. The basic default position for meetings, with very few exceptions, will be discernment by consensus process. There will be process; it will not be the "consensus" we sometimes see at meetings, including of ourselves, where the chair decides and proclaims consensus, but the process will not be bound by the formalities of parliamentary debate. Everyone involved will need to be trained. Moderators will have a significant role and will need specific training to effectively accompany the process of discerning the emerging consensus. Moderators will be assisted by a recorder charged with the responsibility of tracking the language of emerging consensus. Participants will be given indicator cards and will learn to use them to reflect response to emerging ideas. Instead of voting, there will be a frequent testing of the room as the discussion proceeds.

The process is marked by openness, to exploring ways of looking at ideas and issues, to encouraging reflection. One of the significant results of a decision session that functions according to discernment is the result that concludes that there are various opinions and these various opinions are recorded in the report of the meeting. Some have expressed the concern that the process will be so slow that no decisions will be reached, or that the Council will lose its prophetic voice. Those who have engaged in the process affirm that agendas may need to be streamlined with fewer matters coming to decision, but that the commitment of the body to decisions taken is greatly enhanced. They affirm that the sense of having engaged in a spiritual process of discernment, in fact, gives decisions even more authority and power.

In some cases the business committee may feel that matters need to be decided and the process is at an impasse. There is a process to shift to voting that preserves the right of the body to decide whether in fact it agrees that a decision must be taken and then to move to decision-making by vote in a way that assures the Orthodox churches, and other minorities in the Council, that the process will be fair. There is provision for recording in the minutes of the meeting, the record and reports the opinion of those who do not agree with the decision of the meeting, but who have agreed to give consent that the decision may go forward. Finally, the body may decide to postpone the matter or to agree that no decision can be reached.

Conclusion

Neither the report of the Special Commission generally, nor the shift to consensus process for the conduct of meetings, solves all of the problems of the World Council of Churches. Questions of viability and relevance remain; the financial stability of the Council is not sure. But the one significant piece that has so troubled the Orthodox churches and has for many years inhibited their full participation in the work of the WCC, that is, concern about process that marginalized their ecclesiology and theology, may have been solved.

In this light I would like to repeat the conclusions of Dr Mary Tanner in her remarks to the inter-Orthodox pre-assembly meeting in Rhodes, which bear repeating until they become part of the life and tradition of the WCC:

> The emphasis of the Special Commission on the qualities of life together in a praying and discerning community, seeking consensus on some of the most divisive issues

of the church and the world may just help the fellowship of churches to be a more prophetic community both in what it discerns and the way it goes about that discernment. The church is prophetic both in what it says and also in the way it handles complex issues of faith, justice and peace.[8]

In conclusion, it may be appropriate to recall from several years ago the sermon to the 2002 Faith and Order anniversary celebration in Lausanne offered by His Beatitude Archbishop Anastasios that included the following reassurance:

> As we proceed into the 21st century, with the multitudes of studies and proclamations made by the ecumenical movement, and more especially by the Faith and Order commission on the delicate subject of Christian unity and authentic Christian witness in today's world, we will once again have to emphasise the original and essential foundation of the church, which ensures our cohesion. Put simply it is to trust in him to whom "all authority in heaven and on earth has been given", as well as maintaining our firm faith that the church is "his body, the fullness of him who is filling the universe in all its parts" (Eph. 1:23).[9]

NOTES

[1] Those who have followed closely the reports and articles following the final report of the Special Commission on Orthodox Participation in the WCC will hear echoes of that earlier work and I acknowledge with appreciation the authors of the report of the Special Commission, particularly those on sub-committee 1 who prepared appendix B; the Rev. Dr Konrad Raiser, former general secretary of the WCC, who framed the initial work in response to the recommendation on consensus process; several members of the Special Commission with specific expertise in this area, including Rev. Dr D'Arcy Wood, Eden Grace and Prof. Richard Schneider, as well as Dr Janice Love, who has chaired the committee that is drafting the new rule, and Dr Jill Tabart, who drafted *Coming to Consensus: A Case Study for Churches* (WCC Publications, 2003) and who, with Rev. Dr D'Arcy Wood, prepared the initial draft of the proposed revised rule and the manual that is being developed to assist its use.

[2] Report of the Special Commission on Orthodox Participation in the WCC, §49.

[3] Basis of the World Council of Churches, constitution, article I.

[4] Rev. Dr Konrad Raiser, draft composite report on the consensus method of decision-making, Geneva, June 2003.

[5] Eden Grace, "Guided by the mind of Christ – yearning for a new spirituality of church governance", address to the Amesbury Council of Churches annual meeting, 19 Jan. 2003.

[6] Dr Janice Love, "Doing Democracy Differently", *The Ecumenical Review*, vol. 55, no. 1, 2003, p.74.

[7] Grace, "Guided by the mind of Christ".

[8] Dr Mary Tanner, see her paper in this volume.

[9] Sermon on Matt. 28:18-20 given by Archbishop Dr Anastasios (Yannoulatos) seventy-fifth anniversary of Faith and Order in Lausanne, 2002. http://www.wcc-coe.org/wcc/what/faith/anastasios-e.pdf.

On the Special Commission
on Orthodox Participation in the WCC

The Orthodox Churches, the World Council of Churches,
and the Ecumenical Movement

VERY REV. LEONID KISHKOVSKY

The ecumenical encounter must be based on prayer and intercession for one another. I will therefore begin by reading a prayer attributed to the Elders of Optina, a monastery in Russia. This is not an ancient monastery. Yet in the 19th century it became an authentic spiritual centre. Its elders attracted many people from all walks of life in Russia. Among them were writers, philosophers, religious thinkers. The monastery was closed by the communists for many decades. Some of its elders and monks were killed in the gulag, others suffered exile. After the collapse of the Soviet state in the 1990s, Optina Monastery was returned to the church, and monastic life there is being restored. Here are the words of the prayer. Where the original text speaks only about family members, I am adding "colleagues, co-workers and friends", thus encompassing in the prayer every participant of this conference.

> Lord, grant me to meet in spiritual peace everything which the coming day brings to me. Grant that I may fully accept your holy will. At every hour of this day and in all things teach and support me. Whatever may be the news I receive in the course of the day, teach me to accept them with a calm soul and with the firm conviction that your holy will is in all things.
>
> In all my words and actions guide my thoughts and feelings. In all unforeseen circumstances do not allow me to forget that all are sent down by You.
>
> Teach me to act honestly and wisely with every member of my family, with every colleague, co-worker, and friend, without embarrassing or embittering anyone.
>
> Lord, grant me the strength to endure the fatigue of the coming day, and all events in the course of the day. Guide my will and teach me to pray, to believe, to hope, to be patient, and to love. Amen.

Among theological and historical reflections on the ecumenical movement, the World Council of Churches, and Orthodox participation both in the movement and the Council, an essay by Fr Alexander Schmemann is a particularly valuable contribution. The essay, "Moment of Truth for Orthodoxy", [1] offers a reflection on Orthodox ecumenical participation, with special reference to Orthodox participation and membership in the World Council of Churches. Fr Alexander begins by describing the apparently self-evident positive and optimistic nature of the Orthodox participation, if one bases oneself on official reports and declarations. He points out that *"officially,* the Orthodox participation in the WCC looks like a well-established tradition, raising no questions or doubts". Fr Alexander asks: "… does this official optimism correspond to the real situation?" And he gives a negative answer to this question, pointing out "that there exists a discrepancy between the official Orthodox position in the WCC and the 'real' Orthodoxy, and… that this discrepancy constitutes an urgent issue for the WCC, which, if it is not understood in time, may sooner or later lead to a major ecumenical crisis."

In his analysis, Fr Alexander states that "Orthodox participation in the WCC not only remains an ever open question, but encounters a deeply rooted suspicion and even hostility that cannot be simply ascribed to dead conservatism, lack of interest or mere provincialism". The official position of the Orthodox churches on membership in the WCC, according to Fr Alexander, is "dangerously cut off from not so much the feelings of the 'average' Orthodox, but from Orthodox reality itself, that is the totality of spiritual, theological and liturgical experience which alone can give life and authenticity to the acts of ecclesiastical policy".

Thus, while Orthodox representatives are very much in the WCC, *representation* has not become *participation.*

The reason for this, in Fr Alexander's assessment, is to be found in the orientation and terms of reference of the ecumenical encounter and conversation. For a Western Christian (meaning a Catholic or Protestant Christian), the "central ecumenical problem of unity, division, reunion is formulated mainly in terms of the Catholic-Protestant dichotomy and opposition, for the Orthodox church the fundamental opposition is that between the East and the West, understood as two spiritual and theological 'trends' or 'worlds'".

All of this, in the conviction of Fr Alexander, results in a *fundamentally false position* of the Orthodox church in the WCC. "It is false both theologically and institutionally, and this falsehood explains the constant Orthodox 'agony' in the ecumenical movement, the anxiety and the doubts it raises in the Orthodox consciousness." In the ecumenical movement the Orthodox church was forced into the position of accepting ecumenical presuppositions in terms of the Catholic-Protestant dichotomy. Fr Alexander notes that the "separate Orthodox statements" at major ecumenical conferences repeatedly illustrated the "feeling of being in a false position, which was almost always that of the Orthodox delegates". Finally, the structure of the WCC, due to the Western religious situation, had to be based on the "denominational" principle. Thus, the nature of the divisions within Protestantism became the normative understanding of Christian divisions. As Fr Alexander puts it, "The division between Protestant 'denominations' is radically different in its very nature from the division between Orthodoxy and Protestantism, on the one hand, and Orthodox and Roman Catholicism on the other hand."

The essay of Fr Alexander Schmemann ends with words of warning and hope. "We have reached, it seems to me, the 'moment of truth', and there is a great need for clarity and responsibility. So much has been given to us in the ecumenical encounter, so many wonderful possibilities open. We have no right to betray them."

This essay of Fr Alexander Schmemann was written in the early 1960s, and appears in a volume called *Unity in Mid-Career: An Ecumenical Critique*, published in 1963. During the 1990s, as the deep crisis in the Orthodox participation in the WCC became evident to all, there was a tendency to attribute the crisis to Orthodox "fundamentalism", to misunderstandings and lack of information on the part of Orthodox clergy and laity. Yet, as we have seen, the crisis was anticipated some thirty years earlier. And the reflections on "The Moment of Truth for Orthodoxy" were rooted in theological and historical assessments.

Through the decades signs of Orthodox unease were frequently given. We can even identify the debates which resulted in the famous Toronto Statement (1950) on the "ecclesiological neutrality" of the WCC as an early witness to the difficulties of Orthodox participation in the WCC. At numerous conferences and meetings, the Orthodox representatives felt it necessary to make separate statements, to indicate their discomfort with the methodology, orientation and formulation of WCC positions. The Sofia consultation (1981) – a meeting of the general secretary of the WCC with representatives of the Eastern Orthodox churches – discussed and recorded elements of the Orthodox dissatisfaction with the structure and orientation of the WCC. At the Canberra assembly (1991) a decade later, the Orthodox delegations felt compelled to raise alarms about theological orientations becoming evident in the WCC, including such concerns as syncretism, the weakening of trinitarian language, and departure from the basis of the WCC. As the "anti-ecumenism" in the Orthodox world intensified in the 1990s, the pressures on the hierarchy of the various Orthodox churches increased. A consultation of Eastern Orthodox churches was convened in Thessaloniki in May 1998, resulting in a strong statement of concern and alarm, and a demand to create a special body, on the basis of parity, to assess in depth the crisis faced by the WCC with regard to the continued participation of Orthodox churches. Finally, at the WCC assembly at Harare in December 1998, a Special Commission on Orthodox Participation in the WCC was affirmed. This Special Commission, half of whose members were appointed by the respective Eastern and Oriental Orthodox churches, and half by the central committee of the WCC to represent the other member churches, had the mandate to assess the structure, style and ethos of the WCC.

The timing for the creation of the Special Commission was determined by the "populist anti-ecumenism" which had emerged in the Orthodox churches, especially in Eastern Europe, during the 1990s. During the 1990s the deep crisis in the Orthodox participation in the WCC became evident and unavoidable. With the collapse of the communist regimes in the Soviet Union and in Central and Eastern Europe, public opinion in newly free Orthodox churches became a serious factor in the life and decision-making of the churches. Under the pressure of this public opinion, populist in its expression and anti-ecumenical in its orientation, the churches of Bulgaria and Georgia withdrew from membership in the World Council of Churches. In other Orthodox churches the critique of ecumenical structures and participation, and the WCC in particular, was also growing. This was certainly true of the Moscow Patriarchate and the Church of Greece. It is noteworthy that the critique and rejection of ecumenical participation was also gaining strength among Orthodox in North America.

Against this background, it was easy to attribute the Orthodox critique of ecumenism to "populism" and "fundamentalism", seeing it as a characteristic of the "mood" of the late 20th century. The problem with this assessment was not only its shallowness and inadequacy. The assessment was simply incorrect, given the long history of the ecumenical tensions in the participation of the Orthodox churches in the WCC.

I would like to share a personal story illustrating the ambiguities and public perceptions of Orthodox participation in ecumenical bodies. In the early 1990s I served a term as president of the National Council of the Churches of Christ in the USA. The *New York Times* published a story about the NCCCUSA and my installation as its president. The story itself was accurate in its reporting. The headline for the story announced "Orthodox priest heads Protestant council". It is obvious, of course, that the membership of the NCCCUSA was not Protestant only, and that most of the Orthodox churches in the USA were members as well. Yet there was something revealing both about perceptions and realities in the headline. For many Protestants and Orthodox the NCCCUSA was, indeed, a quintessentially Protestant organization – the membership of the Orthodox churches notwithstanding. And the structures and orientations, the ethos and style of the NCCCUSA were certainly an expression of a Protestant ecumenical enterprise.

After the central committee of the WCC received and approved the report of the Special Commission on Orthodox Participation in the WCC, it is interesting that some leaders of the Evangelical Church in Germany expressed the view that the new direction of the WCC suggested the need for a Protestant ecumenical council. Perhaps this revealed an inner truth – both of perception and of reality – that the ethos and style of the WCC, as well as the content of the WCC's work, reflected Protestant issues and priorities. If, now, the ethos, style and priorities of the WCC were to become equally relevant and equally open to the Orthodox and Protestant member churches, then Protestants might reasonably feel that they were losing something, without being certain of any gain.

Before continuing our consideration of the ecumenical crisis of the 1990s within the WCC, and especially the contribution of the Special Commission, I must strongly emphasize that the lived history of ecumenical life in the WCC without any doubt gives evidence of a genuine exchange of spiritual gifts among and between the Christian East and the Christian West in the context of the ecumenical movement. For example, some years ago, in the early 1980s, Dr William Lazareth, then director of Faith and Order in the WCC, created a text on the icon of the Trinity painted by St Andrew Rublev in Russia in the 14th century. If my recollection is accurate, this text, together with a video presentation, was prepared for the WCC Vancouver assembly. This reflection on the icon of the

Trinity was a profound and insightful meditation, in which a Christian in a Western context both received and shared the insights offered by the icon of the Trinity painted in the Eastern context. A more recent example of the "reception" of Orthodox icons and their spiritual world by Christians of the West is offered by a beautiful book on icons by Rowan Williams, the Archbishop of Canterbury. Orthodox participants in the life of the WCC, and in the broader context of the ecumenical movement, have also received gifts of Christian insight and experience from the churches and traditions of the Christian West.

Such sharing of spiritual and theological gifts has sometimes been cited as proof that the ecumenical crisis of the 1990s was exaggerated. Our references to the "Moment of Truth for Orthodoxy" by Fr Alexander Schmemann demonstrate that the ecumenical crisis was real and was present at the creation of the WCC.

The Special Commission receiving its mandate from the WCC assembly in 1998, worked until 2002. In reflecting on the structure, style and ethos of the WCC, the Commission identified the following themes for its working agenda: ecclesiology, social and ethical issues, common prayer, consensus mode of decision-making, and membership and representation. The recommendations of the Special Commission to the central committee of the WCC on these themes offer the WCC fellowship a new way of being together as churches.

Two important quotations – one the words of the moderator of the central committee, His Holiness Catholicos Aram I, the other from Konrad Raiser, then general secretary of the WCC – illustrate the significance of the Special Commission's contribution to the WCC.

> Never before in its fifty years of history has the WCC taken its Orthodox member churches as seriously.
>
> *Konrad Raiser at the inaugural meeting of the Special Commission*

> The Special Commission was the "first time in the history of the WCC that the two main Christian traditions of East and West have engaged in a comprehensive dialogue on an equal basis".
>
> *Catholicos Aram I at the central committee plenary (2002)*
> *dedicated to the Special Commission report*

The crisis of Orthodox participation in the WCC presented an ecumenical challenge. Through the Special Commission the member churches and the WCC have addressed this challenge and have offered a new way of being together on an equal basis. We now look forward to the ninth assembly in Porto Alegre, Brazil, to receive the recommendations of the Special Commission as presented by the central committee and to give them life and authority in the fellowship of the World Council of Churches.

NOTE

[1] Iin *Unity in Mid-Career: An Ecumenical Critique*, Keith R. Bridston and Walter D. Wagoner eds, New York, Macmillan, 1963, pp.47-56.

A Case Study

BISHOP EBERHARDT RENZ

I was asked to give a short report on a first attempt to discuss concrete questions between Orthodox churches and other member churches of the World Council of Churches (WCC), at a seminar on methodologies in approaching social and ethical issues, held in Morges, Switzerland, in October 2003. I will not give a detailed description of this seminar, but rather my impressions and experiences during those days in Morges.

A visit of a delegation of the WCC to the Russian Orthodox Church in June 2001 met with the two papers which the Russian Orthodox Church (ROC) had issued. Discussions followed about "The Basic Principles of the Attitude of the Russian Orthodox Church towards the Other Christian Confessions" and "The Bases of the Social Concept of the Russian Orthodox Church". The delegation under the leadership of Ms Teny Pirri-Simonian came back with the recommendation that member churches of the WCC should study these papers seriously. The best way would be to do this in the form of seminars with equal Orthodox and "non-Orthodox" participation. This was a follow-up of the decision of the Special Commission to "provide opportunities for the churches to consult with one another, and wherever possible, to speak together". The WCC took the initiative to organize a discussion on social and ethical issues by using the document "Bases of the Social Concept" adopted by the bishops council of the Russian Orthodox Church in 2000 as a principal case study.

The seminar in Morges was a first attempt. From those present here, Metropolitan Anba Bishoy, Fr Mikhail Gundyaev and Dr Peter Bouteneff were participating. It was the first time that representatives of different churches together discussed a case study on one church's social teaching and methodology. The pursuit of discovering why a church has spoken, what kind of mechanism is used, and which are the tools of discernment – this is very much in the spirit of the Special Commission. The WCC attempts to create the "space" for members of the fellowship of churches to consult each other, share the fruits of their deliberations and eventually speak and act together. To practise this was the main purpose of the meeting in Morges.

My conclusion after those days: we need many more such opportunities to discuss certain topics. There is a difference between the bilateral talks with one Protestant church on one side and one Orthodox church on the other side (e.g. bilateral talks of Evangelical Church in Germany (EKD) and Russian Orthodox Church, or EKD and Romanian Orthodox Church). A meeting like the one in Morges brings together representatives from various Orthodox churches, Oriental and Eastern, as well as from various Protestant traditions.

Each day began with a confessional prayer according to either the Protestant or Orthodox tradition.

After an introduction under the theme "Methodologies in approaching social and ethical issues: suggestions for reflection", two papers were presented on each sub-topic, one from the Orthodox participant and the other from a Protestant participant. Four sub-topics were discussed:

- the church and social and political ethics
- the church and problems of bio-ethics and ecology
- the church and personal and public morality
- international relations: problems of globalization

The following are a few impressions which I noted for myself (a Protestant, a Lutheran) as important insights in such conversations and discussions.

1. *Church fathers*
   - It is astonishing how Orthodox churches and theologians use the wisdom of the church fathers, almost more quotations from them than from the Bible.
   - It is astonishing how many great thoughts can be found in the church fathers' reasoning.
   - The question arises why Protestants do not use this treasure of old. The centuries of the church fathers belong to our common church history.
   - I realize of course: Lutherans, for instance, quote Martin Luther all the way as their "church father".
   - What could we all gain in bringing together what we cherish from our own tradition?

2. *Tradition*
   - Metropolitan Bishoy once asked, "Which Tradition do you mean, the one before or the one after Constantine?"
   - For me as a Protestant all that happened since the time of Jesus and the apostles until today is "Tradition", good or bad. It has its weight and is part of Tradition, that is, what has been brought over to me and I have to take this all into consideration for today.

3. *Hermeneutics*
   - How do we understand the Bible? It is very helpful to demonstrate to one another the way, the methods, the instruments, how we arrive at our respective conclusions out of our exegetical work.
   - When we compare our steps, then this forces us to go into details and to make clear, under which conditions (preconditions and presuppositions etc.) we do our work.
   - It is not enough to put different positions against one another, but to make clear in which way we reach this or that position.

4. *Context* or "localness" (with the words of Fr George)
   - Our theological work is always influenced, reflected, moulded in and by a certain time, a certain place, among certain people, with our experiences under certain conditions.

- How far do we take this into consideration as an ongoing process which never ends?

5. *Terminology*
   - We use the same words, but do we mean the same things by them?
   - We have to be precise and we are precise in our thinking, but we use the same words with different concepts out of our respective tradition.
   - Our theological heritage to a certain extent defines our thinking. How far is this "necessary", how far is this a sort of "captivity"?

6. *New language*
   - We Protestants are eager to "invent" new language, but we realize that this can be to the detriment of the content. It can mean a loss of wisdom of old and a loss of being precise.
   - But new questions, changes in our situations force us to find words understandable for those who hear us.
   - We all live in the same reality of today's world. How can we help one another in this respect as Orthodox and "non-Orthodox" Christians?

The Significance of the Special Commission

DR MARY TANNER

I am grateful to have been invited to this inter-Orthodox pre-assembly meeting and to be asked, as an Anglican member of the Special Commission, to speak about its work. In speaking about the Special Commission I think it important to avoid describing myself as a "non-Orthodox" member, as if identity can be described satisfactorily by what we are not.

I have served on many commissions, Anglican and ecumenical, and I can truly say that for me the Special Commission has been one of the most significant, both in terms of its ethos as well as for the conclusions it reached. Both its working style and its conclusions, if taken seriously and implemented, could have a profound influence on the ecumenical movement of the next years. It was, however, by no means clear that this would be the case when we gathered for our first meeting and listened to our Orthodox co-chairman, Metropolitan Chrysostomos of Ephesus, review the reasons that had led two Orthodox churches to leave the Council and others to be nearing that point. The task was an urgent one, agreed His Holiness Aram I, for the Orthodox had not been able to integrate their concerns into the ecumenical agenda. While he acknowledged that you could not afford to retreat into parochialism, neither could Protestant churches afford to impose on you an ecumenical agenda that may sooner or later lead to the disintegration of the Council. He challenged the Commission: "Let us reshape and restructure the Council by redefining our perceptions and rearticulating our vision more clearly, and by setting the kind of decision-making procedures and working agenda that respond to the expectations and needs of our churches."

A changed ethos

First a few words about the ethos and style of the meetings that developed in the life of the Commission in its four main meetings, held between 1999 and 2002, as well as in meetings of small groups considering special issues. The meetings, with an equal number of Orthodox representatives (Eastern and Oriental) and half representatives from the other member churches of the WCC, came to be characterized by honest speaking and intense listening to one another, the sort of listening which really struggles to hear what the other person is saying and tries to see issues through the eyes of the other. Of course, there were painful times of plain speaking and of withdrawal into two groups. But it quickly became apparent that it was not a matter of you the Orthodox and the rest of us on different sides; there was a spectrum of opinions on most issues which hardly ever followed two lines of thought, Orthodox and the rest. And, although the Commission had been set up to listen to your Orthodox concerns about the Council, its agenda, its style of working, its imbalance of membership, in fact many of your issues and perspectives were quickly seen to be shared by others around the table. The Special Commission was, therefore, an opportunity for all. As an Anglican I was grateful that some of the matters placed on the table by the Orthodox included those which Anglicans had raised within the context of the Common Understanding and Vision process before the Harare assembly. Here was a chance to look at these issues again, this time with a greater seriousness than it seemed the CUV process had provided us with.

It is impossible to talk about the ethos of the meetings without referring to the opportunities the Commission was given to meet in a number of different Orthodox contexts, which enabled us to experience at first hand the life of different Orthodox churches – in Egypt, Crete, Cyprus, Thessalonica and, most recently, in Belarus. In all of these places we were welcomed by local congregations and received with immense generosity. This experience opened up for many of us from the other member churches a window into Orthodox spirituality, theology and faithful Christian witness at the local level which helped us to get hold at a deeper level of some of the theological and organizational concerns that were being addressed around the table. For this enriching experience we owed a huge debt to Yorgo Lemopoulos and the WCC staff for their imaginative planning of meetings and to the churches and students who welcomed us and interpreted for us their unique contexts.

I hope that this is enough to convey to you something of the spirit of the meetings and the real "fellowship in discernment" that came to be experienced by this group with its parity of Orthodox and those from other member churches of the WCC, searching together for the most creative way forward in the future for the privileged instrument of the World Council of Churches. The Commission did become a fellowship in discernment, respecting difference and prepared to explore difference. This meant for many of us that we never saw our own views in quite the same way again.

Two fundamental issues

Let me turn now to the discoveries of the Commission.[1] The introduction to the final report of the Special Commission underlines two basic understandings about the identity of the World Council of Churches. These require a "mind-shift" in the understanding of every member church, Orthodox and the rest, if the Council is, in the future, to function for us all.

- First, the Council has to be understood by all of us and, not least of all by the staff and officers of the Council, as a "fellowship of churches" and *not* some independent entity standing over against the churches. It is a fellowship of churches that seeks, at the heart of all it does, the visible unity of the one, holy, catholic and apostolic church. Moreover, it is the churches themselves that teach and make doctrinal, moral and ethical decisions and not the Council over against the churches. It is the churches that proclaim consensus and not the Council. The Council may act as a midwife in helping the churches towards consensus but it cannot proclaim doctrinal consensus on behalf of the churches.

- Second, the Council is an instrument which gathers churches in an "ecumenical space", where churches themselves can decide their common agenda, undertake activities of all sorts together in the arenas of justice, peace and the preservation of creation, and, through dialogue, break down barriers that divide them. The Council is not a structure which undertakes its own agenda or activities apart from the churches.

When these two fundamental understandings about the Council are grasped they have huge consequences for addressing all of the concerns raised by the Orthodox, about membership, agenda and styles of working.

Five areas of exploration and recommendation

In the light of these two general reflections the report of the Special Commission sets out its reflections on five main areas:

1. Ecclesiology

It is significant that ecclesiology was put first. The Commission saw that issues of ecclesiology, issues relating to "the nature and purpose of the church", lie behind almost all that the Commission discussed. It is important for all of us to keep on exploring whether those in the fellowship share a common understanding of what it means to be church and whether we share an understanding of the visible unity of the church, which lies at the heart of our common calling.The report asks sharply: How do we understand the call to visible unity and how can we claim and receive together work we have already done on visible unity? We do not have to begin our reflections on the church and its unity from scratch. We have a common heritage in the work of Faith and Order, work that is greatly indebted to the contribution of Orthodox scholars, not least among them Nikos Nissiotis and John Zizioulas. Together the member churches have crafted and adopted over the years assembly statements on the unity of the church. Nevertheless, the question remains, have our churches owned our common ecclesiological work?

The report of the Special Commission poses a sharp ecclesiological question to the Orthodox churches: Is there room in your ecclesiology for other churches? This is a telling question and puts its finger on the question many who are from other member churches really do want to know, namely, whether the Orthodox regard themselves as the only true church and whether you are able to recognize some form of "ecclesial reality", some form of ecclesiological significance, some elements of church in other churches. The way this question is answered will, to a large extent, affect the way a church participates in the ecumenical movement, as well as its attitude to other churches who understand themselves as only a part of the one, holy, catholic and apostolic church.

Those of us who are not Orthodox really do need to hear what the Orthodox have to say to us about the deep experiences we share together with you and what estimate you make of these experiences. When, for example, I take part with you, as I did in the morning office this morning, when I pray with you to the Father, joined in Christ, through the power of the Holy Spirit, how should I talk of our shared experience of being joined in the life and love of God? Or because I am baptized by water in the name of the Father, and of the Son, and of the Holy Spirit, and have died with Christ and risen to new life in him, what sort of relationship has God, in his grace, established between us? You Orthodox have given many of us, in bilateral and multilateral conversations, the confidence to use the language of koinonia. You have helped us to understand that koinonia expresses the deepest truth about the being of the church and about our life in Christ. If we have sometimes used the language carelessly, you the Orthodox must help to correct us. I struggle to find a language that will do justice to explaining something of the life we already share. I find "degrees of communion" unhelpful, but neither can I simply say "we are out of communion"; juridically that is so, but spiritually surely there is more that can be claimed. Can we then speak of "partial communion" or "restricted communion"? This is a discussion we must all have together.

The Special Commission saw that there was not only a question to be put to the Orthodox. There is also a question the Orthodox want to ask of the other churches: How do you understand, maintain and express your belonging to the one, holy, catholic and apostolic church?

These two sharp questions, the one addressed to the Orthodox and the other to the other member churches, get right to the heart of the ecclesiological problem and are related to the current ecumenical confusion. It is time they were handled imaginatively in order that churches within the fellowship can build trust in one another. It may be that the current ecclesiological study in Faith and Order,

The Nature and Purpose of the Church, may provide a context for a creative exploration of these sharp questions.

2. Social and ethical issues

The report of the Special Commission recognizes that the WCC is an important arena in which member churches can, and should, explore ethical issues together. There is no suggestion made by the Commission that the agenda of the Council should be limited or censored by some members. There was a reconciling moment in the life of the Commission when one Orthodox participant made it clear that there was no problem in discussing, for example, the controversial issue of women's ordination as long as the Orthodox perspective is heard and any resulting report reflects fairly that perspective, rather than appearing to adopt only one position on the matter. What the report does ask for is that holy scripture and the church's Tradition be taken more seriously in approaching ethical issues, that there should also be greater clarity on the methodology used in approaching social and ethical issues, and that space should be given for all voices around the table to be heard and diverse opinions registered, with attention given to both majority and minority voices. Further, it should always be made clear that it is not the WCC that takes decisions in moral and ethical issues, but the member churches themselves. Authority remains with the churches. The function of the WCC is to provide a unique forum, a space, in which views can be exchanged, insights gained from the experience of others, and opinions formed in conversation with one another.

3. Common prayer

This, in many ways, turned out to be the most sensitive part of the Special Commission's work and, not surprisingly, has proved the most controversial. The Commission affirmed that prayer is essential to the ecumenical movement. Common prayer must continue to be the foundation of the ecumenical endeavour and the life blood of ecumenical relations. There can be no ecumenical movement without common prayer. There is no giving up on that. All ecumenical activities are rooted in prayer. There is, however, in the report a move away from the description of prayer in ecumenical contexts as "ecumenical worship", as if there was some special form of worship that can be branded as "ecumenical worship". The word "worship" is, we came to see, ambiguous. Those of us who are not Orthodox had to take on board that for you, the Orthodox, "worship" implies the liturgy, eucharistic worship.

In the ecumenical movement we are not looking for some other category of prayer that can be characterized as "ecumenical worship", as distinct from ecclesial worship. In the ecumenical fellowship of churches we are committed to praying together, we are committed to engaging together in common prayer. In doing this we may offer to one another the riches of our own tradition, using the Anglican, or Methodist, or Orthodox, or Quaker tradition of prayer. In such cases the prayer would be led by the appropriate person in that tradition – a man or a woman, lay or ordained – according to the custom of the particular tradition hosting the prayer. On such occasions one tradition might actually choose to celebrate a eucharist, applying its own discipline of eucharistic hospitality. It would need to be made clear that the celebration was a part of the living tradition of a particular church, which was being offered. This would not be an "ecumenical liturgy", there is no such thing as an "ecumenical liturgy", but rather the liturgy of a particular ecclesial tradition to which others are invited to take an appropriate part. The experience of the richness of other traditions is an important element in the ecumenical movement and it may well be that the tendency in the past has been to move too quickly away from offering the experience of worship of authentic ecclesial traditions in favour of a mixed and impoverished experience. The response to such invitations by particular churches would be governed for each person present by the discipline of his or her own church and by their conscience. And all would respect the different disciplines of others.

In addition to offering the riches of particular traditions for all to experience, the Commission also recommended that in ecumenical gatherings elements from different traditions should at times be brought together in what it termed "interconfessional prayer". The drawing up of guidelines for "interconfessional prayer" will be an important and delicate task for the future. An appendix to the report of the Commission provides a framework for common prayer at ecumenical meetings. There is more work to be done in developing those guidelines.

This careful distinction of two types of common prayer which can be encouraged in ecumenical contexts avoids the use of the term "worship". It also avoids the notion that the ecumenical community is trying to model a new form of worship for a super church "in becoming". If these suggestions for worship from the Special Commission are adopted it would mean, and some Protestant churches have found this hard, that there would be no future celebrations of a so called "ecumenical liturgy" like the Lima liturgy. However, if a particular church had already, as some have done, adopted the Lima liturgy as an authoritative liturgical text for its own use, then that church might wish to offer the Lima liturgy as its own form of eucharistic liturgy. It would need to be understood that this is not an "ecumenical eucharist" but the eucharist of the church to which the presiding minister belongs. Any offering of eucharistic hospitality would come from that church and not from the ecumenical fellowship and be in accordance with that church's discipline. Any response to an invitation would be made by individuals according to the discipline of their own church informed by their own conscience.

4. *Consensus decision-making*

The Special Commission recommended that the WCC should move from a parliamentary style of debate and voting, where simple majorities carry the day and minorities are over-ruled, to a process of discerning the mind of Christ under the guidance of the Holy Spirit, in which the views of all are taken into consideration.[2] It may be that it was unhelpful to use the phrase "consensus decision-making", with its bringing together of the notions of consensus and decision-making. To talk of consensus discernment gets better at the heart of what the Commission offers. In consensus discernment different views on a matter are carefully and respectfully heard and recorded. Under a skillful moderator the mind of the group is discerned and drawn out. Different forms of consensus were identified by the Commission. Consensus is reached where unanimity on a subject is reached; or where the minority agrees to go with the majority; or where it is agreed by all to take no action; or where a consensus statement records all opinions faithfully and leaves the matter open for future reflection. Consensus discernment never rules a minority out of court. Moving to a model of consensus discernment will require great skill on the part of moderators, as well as an understanding by the community of the processes of consensus discernment. It is a way of discernment that requires a new ethos and culture, a change of attitudes to one another. The Special Commission experienced something of this way of working in its own style of working which convinced members of the Commission that it is possible to change the culture and ways of working within the fellowship of churches in the WCC.

Consensus discernment does not, however, mean that there are no issues which require a voting procedure. Clearly, an organization cannot function without being able to take certain decisions, particularly in those practical concerns which govern the life of the organization, for example resourcing and staffing. Some issues will need to be addressed on a parliamentary style for the organization to function smoothly. However, it is likely that far fewer areas will require this old method than is sometimes thought.

The Special Commission offers a creative way forward in its suggestions around consensus discernment though there is still work to be done in understanding consensus discernment, and communicating it more widely.

Attention was given to the idea of parity between the Orthodox and others in discernment and decision-making, which led to the suggestion that there should be a Permanent Committee on Consensus and Collaboration made up of 50 percent Orthodox and 50 percent other member churches. Its brief would include continuing the work of the Special Commission and giving advice on proposed agenda items. Work is already in hand to develop this proposal to be put into practice following the assembly in Porto Alegre.

5. Membership

The Special Commission recommended that in future there should be two distinct ways of relating to the WCC: the first "member churches belonging to the fellowship"; second, "churches in association", churches with the right to speak at meetings but not to vote. This second category might serve as a "resting place" while churches considered whether to apply for full membership or in which to rest while considering withdrawing from the membership of the Council. In an appendix to its report the Special Commission sets out criteria for churches applying to join the WCC, including theological criteria: a church must profess faith in the triune God expressed in the scriptures and the Nicene-Constantinopolitan Creed; baptize in the name of the Father, Son and Holy Spirit, and acknowledge the need to move towards the recognition of the baptism of other churches; recognize the presence and activity of Christ and the Holy Spirit outside its own boundaries; and recognize in other member churches elements of the true church, even if it does not recognize them as churches in the true and full sense of the word. If we were all able to accept such criteria there would be a new confidence in the life and work of the fellowship of churches in the WCC.

Final reflections

The Special Commission has not come up with a blueprint for the Council of the future. It has identified five areas for change. If these meet with a positive response there would be significant change in the ethos, working style and agenda of the Council for good. It should result in a stronger and more credible ecumenical instrument at the world level in which not only the Orthodox but all of us would have greater confidence. It would be more faithful to the vision and perspectives of the founding movements and would strengthen our commitment to our common calling to work for the visible unity of the church in one faith and one eucharistic fellowship, in service and mission, an inseparable agenda. It might make the WCC a more attractive ecumenical instrument for other churches, not least the Roman Catholic and Pentecostal churches. How such a reformed, privileged instrument of the ecumenical movement would serve the one ecumenical movement requires thought within the discussions around the "reconfiguration" of the ecumenical movement. It would be a missed opportunity if the discussions about the "reformed" life of the WCC, made in the report of the Special Commission, are separated from the wider discussions about the whole ecumenical movement. Discussions around reconfiguration make the work of the Special Commission more relevant and not less.

Finally, the work of the Special Commission may seem at first sight to be a luxury, simply about Christians looking inward at their own narrow concerns. I do not believe that this is so. For the way we live together as we move from separation towards visible unity is both a sign of the unity we believe God is calling us to live together, that manifestation in this life of God's own life of communion, and also a sign to the world of its own possibility. The emphasis of the Special Commission on the qualities of life together in a praying and discerning community, seeking consensus on some of the most divisive issues of the church and the world, may just help the fellowship of churches to be a more prophetic community both in what it discerns and the way it goes about that discernment. The church is prophetic both in what it says and also in the way it handles complex issues of faith, justice and peace.

I am grateful to the Orthodox for having raised hard questions about our life together in the fellowship of churches. They have opened up for us creative possibilities for the future. I hope that the next assembly, and beyond that, the new officers and leaders of the Council, will understand the promise contained in the proposals of the Special Commission and develop them further.

NOTES

[1] The final Report of the Special Commission on Orthodox Participation in the WCC, *The Ecumenical Review*. Vol. 55, No. 1, January 2003, pp 4-38.
[2] See the paper of Anne Glynn-Mackoul for an in-depth discussion of consensus.

Orthodox Pre-assembly Meeting Affirms the Need for Spiritual Transformation

The spiritual dimensions of transformation underlie the social, observed participants at an international pre-assembly meeting of Orthodox member churches of the World Council of Churches, which completed its work on the island of Rhodes, Greece, yesterday.

In a comprehensive report produced by participants coming from nearly all of the WCC's Eastern Orthodox and Oriental Orthodox member churches, the group outlined its theological contribution and hopes for the WCC's ninth assembly, which will be held in Brazil in early 2006, under the theme, "God, in Your Grace, Transform the World".

The gathering, which involved more than fifty hierarchs, theologians as well as participants from other WCC member churches, was hosted by Metropolitan Kyrillos of Rhodes on behalf of the Ecumenical Patriarchate, 10-17 January 2005. Metropolitan Gennadios of Sassima (Ecumenical Patriarchate) and Metropolitan Bishoy of Damiette (Coptic Orthodox Church) co-chaired the event. Along with the presentation of a series of theological papers, the programme included prayer, meditations and visits to local communities and monasteries.

The pre-assembly of the Eastern Orthodox and Oriental Orthodox churches is traditionally held prior to the WCC's assemblies, which meet every seven years. There are twenty-two Eastern Orthodox and Oriental Orthodox member churches of the WCC, whose combined membership makes up almost half of the Council's total constituency.

Transformation and transfiguration

For the Orthodox, grace is associated with the transforming action of the Holy Spirit in creation. "God's divine unconditional graceful love draws us to him (Rom. 5:15), because humans are not only created by God but they are created *for* God. In God we entirely find the purpose of our lives restored and transformed." The transfiguration of Christ reveals God's ultimate intention for humanity and creation. "Christ gathers all things in him, and the whole of creation is transformed into a new heaven and a new earth."

Spiritual and social transformation are inter-related, the report emphasizes. "The process of the transfiguration of our socio-economic order… involves our personal and communal commitment" and the struggle to forge a "chain of good" affecting all aspects of human life.

Recognizing the suffering, violence, injustice and immorality so evident in the world, the participants expressed their conviction that the task of Christians is to call on the action of the Holy Spirit and to act as "fellow-workers" in restoring the "true humanity created in God's image".

A renewed council, a renewed commitment

The pre-assembly rearticulated the principles undergirding a continued Orthodox commitment to Christian unity. Referring to ongoing discussions about possible new forms of international ecumenical work, the report affirms that "the world will continue to need a council of churches… an instrument to serve the churches by bringing them into a space for dialogue, shared work, for the mutual exchange of gifts and insights from our traditions, for prayer together".

Participants recognized that "ecclesiology is central to the different understandings of Christian division and Christian unity, and therefore the key to our different approaches to the WCC". The status of other churches in Orthodox self-understanding remains one of the most delicate issues affecting Orthodox participation in the ecumenical movement, and the pre-assembly appealed for further serious study in this area.

The Special Commission – a "great promise" for the fellowship

The pre-assembly reviewed the results of the Special Commission on Orthodox participation in the WCC, established by the eighth assembly in 1998 to address Orthodox grievances with the direction and priorities of the Council. It underlined the central importance of the Special Commission's findings which bear "great promise for the whole fellowship" and urged WCC member churches to continue to work on receiving the report, which proposes a series of key reforms to the Council to be presented to the next assembly.

In February 2005, the WCC central committee will consider adopting a new method of consensus decision-making as an alternative to the current majority-vote system. "Introduction of consensus… offers the Council a way to reflect the centrality of holy scripture in its life and engage the work of the Council in an atmosphere of openness, trust and humility [and] will enhance the potential for the Council to find its true prophetic voice," the report stated.

But the pre-assembly report acknowledged that the Orthodox churches are faced both with a moment of opportunity and of particular responsibility as a result of the Special Commission, and calls on the Orthodox churches "to continue to make credible expressions of [their] commitment in the character of [their] participation at every level".

A prayerful contribution

The report culminates in the form of a meditation, which is inspired by the theme of the WCC ninth assembly. The text, drafted as a contribution to the assembly, explores the themes of grace and transformation, and concludes on a note of hope in God: "in your grace, you have given us a glorious world – in us it has fallen, in us let it be raised again".

List of Participants

Host

H.E. Metropolitan Kyrillos of Rhodes
Holy Metropolis of Rhodes
851 00 Rhodes, Greece
Tel/fax: + 30.224.10.23274

Local staff

Fr Emmanuel Sklivakis
Deacon Ioanikos Anagnostou
Deacon Timotheos Apostolakis
Deacon Kirillos Papanthimou
Deacon Achilles Stavroulakis
Mr Konstantinos Hatzimihail

Participants

**H.G. Bishop Dr Athanasios
(Chatzopoulos) of Achaia**
Church of Greece
Representation Office
of the Church of Greece
Bld Saint-Michel 50
1040 Brussels, Belgium
Work tel: +32.2.280.06.39
Work fax:+32.2.280.02.99
E-mail: ecclesiagr@skynet.be

H.G. Bishop Nareg Alemezian
Armenian Apostolic Church
(Holy See of Cilicia)
P.O. Box 70 317
Antelias, Lebanon
Work tel: +961.4.410.001/3
Work fax:+961.4.417.971
E-mail: ecumcil@cathcil.org

**H.E. Archbishop Aristarchos
of Constantine**
Greek Orthodox Patriarchate of Jerusalem
P.O. Box 14234
Jerusalem 91140, Israel
Work tel: +972.2.627.4941
Work fax:+972.2.628.5636
Mobile: +972.522.37.5702
E-mail : aristarch@netvision.net.il

**H.G. Bishop Dr Basilios of Trimithus
(Karayiannis)**
Church of Cyprus
Holy Archbishopric
P.O. Box 21 130
1502 Nicosia, Cyprus
Work tel: +357.22.554.600
Work fax:+357.22.436.079
E-mail: trimith@logos.cy.net

**H.E. Metropolitan Anba Bishoy
of Damiette**
Coptic Orthodox Church
St Mark's Cathedral
222 Ramses Street, Abbassia
Cairo, Egypt
Work tel: +20.2.339.45.04, +20.2.683.02.47
Work fax:+20.5.076.30.08, +20.2.683.66.91
E-mail: demiana@tecmina.com

Rev. Joseph (Leandro Oscar) Bosch
Ecumenical Patriarchate
Via Carlo Cattaneo 2
I-00185 Rome, Italy
Work tel: +39.06.448.698.45
or +39.340.067.11.06
Work fax:+39.06.498.698.32
E-mail: iosifbosch@hotmail.com

Dr Peter Bouteneff
Orthodox Church in America
St Vladimir's Orthodox Theological
Seminary
575 Scarsdale Road
Crestwood, NY 10707, USA
Work tel: +1.914.961.8313
Work fax:+1.914.961.4507
E-mail: pcb@svots.edu

Very Rev. Prof. Emmanuel Clapsis
Greek Orthodox Archdiocese of America/
Ecumenical Patriarchate
Holy Cross Greek Orthodox
School of Theology
50 Goddard Avenue
Brookline, MA 02445, USA
Work tel: +1.617.850.12.12
Work fax:+1.617.850.14.60
E-mail: eclapsis@hchc.edu

**H.E. Metropolitan Prof. Dr Gennadios
of Sassima**
Ecumenical Patriarchate
Rum Patrikhanesi
Fener-Haliç
TR- 34220 Istanbul, Turkey
Work tel: +90.212.531.96.70.76
Work fax:+90.212.531.96.79
E-mail: gennad@attglobal.net

Rev. Dr Kondothra M. George
Malankara Orthodox Syrian Church
The Orthodox Theological Seminary
P.O. Box 98, Kottayam – 686 001
Kerala, India
Work tel: +91.481.2566.526
Work fax:+91.481.2302.571
E-mail: frkmgeorge@hotmail.com

Ms Anne Glynn-Mackoul
Greek Orthodox Patriarchate of Antioch
and All the East
25 Gallup Road
Princeton, NJ 08540, USA
Work tel: +1.609.924.60.47
Work fax:+1.609.279.14.54
E-mail: aglynnmac@worldnet.att.net

Rev. Mikhail Gundyaev
Russian Orthodox Church
150, route de Ferney
P.O. Box 2100
1211 Geneva 2, Switzerland
Work tel: +41.22.791.63.27
Work fax:+41.22.791.63.29
E-mail: mprgeneva@bluewin.ch

Dr Nahed Fahim Habashy
Coptic Orthodox Church c/o Bless
P.O. Box 4019 – Nasr City
Cairo, Egypt
Work tel: +20.2.401.6202
Work fax:+20.2.401.6202
E-mail: nahed_13@yahoo.com

Very Rev. Archimandrite Arsenios
(Jorma) Heikkinen
Orthodox Church of Finland
Address: Suokatu 41 A28
70110 Kuopio, Finland
Work tel: +358.17.287.22.30
Work fax:+358.17.287.22.31
E-mail: piispa.arseni@ort.fi

Dr Sergej Hovorun
Russian Orthodox Church
Danilovsky Monastery
Danilovsky Val 22
113 191 Moscow
Russian Federation
Work tel: +7.095.955.67.75
Work fax:+7.095.230.26.19
E-mail: hovorun@hotmail.com

Very Rev. Archimandrite Benedict Ioannou
Ecumenical Patriarchate
150, route de Ferney
P.O. Box 2100
1211 Geneva 2, Switzerland
Work tel: +41.22.791.63.47
Work fax:+41.22.791.63.46
E-mail: ecupatria@wcc-coe.org

Rev. Prof. Dr Viorel Ionita
Romanian Orthodox Church
Address: Conference of European Churches
150, route de Ferney
P.O. Box 2100
1211 Geneva 2, Switzerland
Work tel: +41.22.791.62.29
Work fax:+41.22.791.62.27
E-mail: vio@cec-kek.org

Ms Katerina Karkala-Zorba
Church of Greece
Kassaveti 147
38 221 Volos, Greece
Work tel: +30.242.10.61.700
Work fax:+30.242.10.61.700
E-mail: women@imd.gr

Mr Stephen W. Kinyanjui
Greek Orthodox Patriarchate of Alexandria
and All Africa
Syndesmos representative
P.O. Box 21026
Adams Arcade
Nairobi, Kenya
Work tel: +254.722.762.619,
or +254.720.778.402
E-mail: widecolours@yahoo.com

Very Rev. Leonid Kishkovsky
Orthodox Church in America
Willow Shore Avenue
Sea Cliff, NY 11579, USA
Work tel: +1.516.922.0550
Work fax:+1.516.922.0954
E-mail: leonid@oca.org

Prof. Dr Dimitra Koukoura
Ecumenical Patriarchate
37, Vas. Konstantinou Ave.
54 622 Thessaloniki, Greece
Work tel/fax: +30.2310.233.953
E-mail: dimkou@theo.auth.gr

Very Rev. Deacon Dr Elpidophoros Lambriniadis
Ecumenical Patriarchate
Rum Patrikhanesi
Fener-Haliç
TR-34220 Istanbul, Turkey
Work tel: +90.212.531.96.74
Work fax:+90.212.531.65.33
E-mail: elpidof@attglobal.net

Dr John Lappas
Orthodox Autocephalous Church
of Albania
72 Agion Ioannou Theologou
GR-155 61 Athens, Greece
Work tel: +30.210.652.5091
Work fax:+355.4.232.109
E-mail:
OrthodoxChurchAlb@ocual.tirana.al

Rev. Prof. Vasile Mihoc
Romanian Orthodox Church
Emile Zola str. 28
RO-550 227 Sibiu, Romania
Home tel: +40.269.239.473
Mobile tel:+40.744.787.293
Work fax:+40.269.216.914
E-mail: mihoc@rdslink.ro

Mr John Ngige Njoroge
Greek Orthodox Patriarchate of Alexandria
and All Africa
St Cyril – Methodius,
Ekklesiastiacu Lykio
Venizelou 51
61 100 Kilkis, Greece
Work tel: +30.697.547.4228
Work fax:+30.234.102.8625
E-mail: ngigenjoroge@yahoo.com

H.E. Archbishop Dr Nifon of Targoviste
Romanian Orthodox Church
str. Mihai Bravu nr. 8
RO-130 004 Targoviste
Jud. Dâmbovita, Romania
Work tel: +40.245.21.37.13,
+40.245.21.15.88
Work fax:+40.245.21.15.88
E-mail: ips_nifon@yahoo.com

Ms Katerina Pastukhova
Russian Orthodox Church/Belarussian
Exarchate
150, route de Ferney
P.O. Box 2100
1211 Geneva 2, Switzerland
Work tel: +41.22.791.60.45
Work fax: +41.22.791.64.07
E-mail: kpa@wcc-coe.org

H.G. Bishop Dr Yeznik Petrossian
Armenian Apostolic Church
(Holy See of Etchmiadzin)
Holy See of Etchmiadzin
Etchmiadzin 378310, Armenia
Work tel:+374.1.517.155, 517.160
Work fax:+374.1.517.301.517.302
E-mail: inter@etchmiadzin.am

H.E. Mor Theophilus George Saliba
Syrian Orthodox Patriarchate of Antioch
and All the East
Syrian Orthodox Archbishop
of Mount Lebanon
P.O. Box 90420
Bouchrieh, Lebanon
Work tel:+961.1.69.03.12/3
Work fax:+961.1.69.03.14
E-mail: bgsaliba@dm.net.lb

Rev. Mihran (Nerseh) Shekhoukian
Armenian Apostolic Church
(Holy See of Cilicia)
P.O. Box 70 317
Antelias, Lebanon
Work tel:+961.4.410.001
Work fax:+961.4.417.971
E-mail: ecumcil@cathcil.org

Ms Carla Siranoussian
Armenian Apostolic Church
(Holy See of Cilicia)
P.O. Box 70 317
Antelias, Lebanon
Work tel:+961.3.257.820
Work fax:+961.1.898.906
E-mail: pertousha@hotmail.com

Rev. Pawel Stefanowski
Autocephalous Orthodox Church of Poland
ul. Boguseada 14/6
70 441 Szczecin, Poland
Work tel: +48.91.434.5008,
+48.601.781.356
Work fax: +48.91.434.5008
E-mail: stefanowski@cerkiew.szczecin.pl

Abba Samuel Wolde Tekestebirhan
Ethiopian Orthodox Tewahedo Church
P O Box 31245
Addis Abeba, Ethiopia
Work tel.: +251.1.56.32.87
Work fax: +251.1.55.22.11
E-mail: aadiosec@telecom.net.et

Ms Outi Vasko
Orthodox Church of Finland
Syndesmos representative
Koulukatu 10 A 4
80110 Joensuu, Finland
Work tel: +358.40.588.96.47
Work fax: +358.13.127.441
E-mail: vasko@cc.joensuu.fi

Rev. Igor Vyzhanov
Russian Orthodox Church
Danilov Monastery
Danilovsky Val 22
113 191 Moscow
Russian Federation
Work tel:+7.095.230.20.94
Work fax:+7.095.230.26.19
E-mail: ivyzhanov@mail.ru

Fraternal participants

Bishop Eberhardt Renz
Evangelical Church in Württemberg (EKD)
Im Alten Rauns 13
DE-72072 Tübingen, Germany
Work tel:+49.7071.70.77.15
Work fax:+49.7071.70.77.18
E-mail: Eberhardtrenz@aol.com

Dr Mary Tanner
Church of England
Camp End Road
St George's Hill
Weybridge, Surrey KT13 0NW
United Kingdom
Work tel:+44.1932.84.27.86
Work fax:+44.171.898.13.69
E-mail: marytanner@tesco.net

WCC staff

Route de Ferney 150
P.O. Box 2100
CH-1211 Geneva 2, Switzerland

Mr Georges Lemopoulos
Deputy General Secretary
Work tel:+41.22.791.62.88
Work fax:+41.22.791.6535
E-mail: yl@wcc-coe.org

Mr Alexander Belopopsky
Team Coordination on Communication
Work tel:+41.22.791.6210
Work fax:+41.22.791.6201
E-mail: alx@wcc-coe.org

Dr Doug Chial
Ninth WCC Assembly Coordinator
Work tel: +41.22.791.6202
Work fax: +41.22.788.00.67
E-mail: dlc@wcc-coe.org

Dr Tamara Grdzelidze
Executive Secretary (Faith and Order)
Work tel:+ 41.22.791.63.39
Work fax:+ 41.22.791.64.07
E-mail: tgr@wcc-coe.org

Dr Tarek Mitri
Programme Executive
Interreligious Dialogue
Work tel: +41.22.791.61.43
Work fax: +41.44.791.61.22
E-mail: tm@wcc-coe.org

Ms Teny Pirri-Simonian
Programme Executive
Church & Ecumenical Relations
General Secretariat
Work tel:+41.22.791.62.04
Work fax:+41.22.788.00.67
E-mail: tps@wcc-coe.org

Rev. Dr Ioan Sauca
Director
Ecumenical Institute of Bossey
Chemin de Chenevière 2
Bogis-Bossey
CH-1298 Céligny, Switzerland
Work tel:+41.22.960.93.28
Work fax:+41.22.776.01.69
E-mail: ios@wcc-coe.org

Ms Renate Sbeghen
Co-opted staff
Ch. François Lehmann 24
1218 Grand Saconnex / GE
Switzerland
Home tel: +41.22.798.42.40
E-mail: r.sbeghen@bluewin.ch

Ms Luzia Wehrle
Administrative Assistant
Church & Ecumenical Relations
General Secretariat
Work tel: +41.22.791.62.03
Work fax:+41.22.788.00.67
E-mail: lmw@wcc-coe.org

Apologies

Dr Agnes Abuom
Anglican Church of Kenya

H.E. Metropolitan Ambrosius of Helsinki
Orthodox Church of Finland

H.G. Bishop Dr Hilarion Alfeyev
Russian Orthodox Church

H.G. Bishop Vicken Aykazian
Armenian Apostolic Church
(Holy See of Etchmiadzin)

H.E. Archbishop Elia Bahi
Syrian Orthodox Patriarchate of Antioch
and All the East

Ms Deborah Belonick
Orthodox Church in America

H.G. Bishop Dr Irinej of Backa
(Mirko Bulovic)
Serbian Orthodox Church

Ms Tamar Karasu
Armenian Patriarchate

Dr Eleni Kasselouri-Hatzivassiliadi
Church of Greece

Bishop Dr Rolf Koppe
Evangelical Church in Germany

Dr Janice Love
United Methodist Church

**H.E. Archbishop Dr Makarios of Kenya
and Irinoupolis**
Greek Orthodox Patriarchate of Alexandria
and All Africa

Ms Margarita Nelyubova
Russian Orthodox Church

H.G. Bishop Serapion
Coptic Orthodox Church

Ms Iveta Starcova
Orthodox Church of the Czech Lands
and Slovakia

Mother Superior Theoxeni
Ecumenical Patriarchate